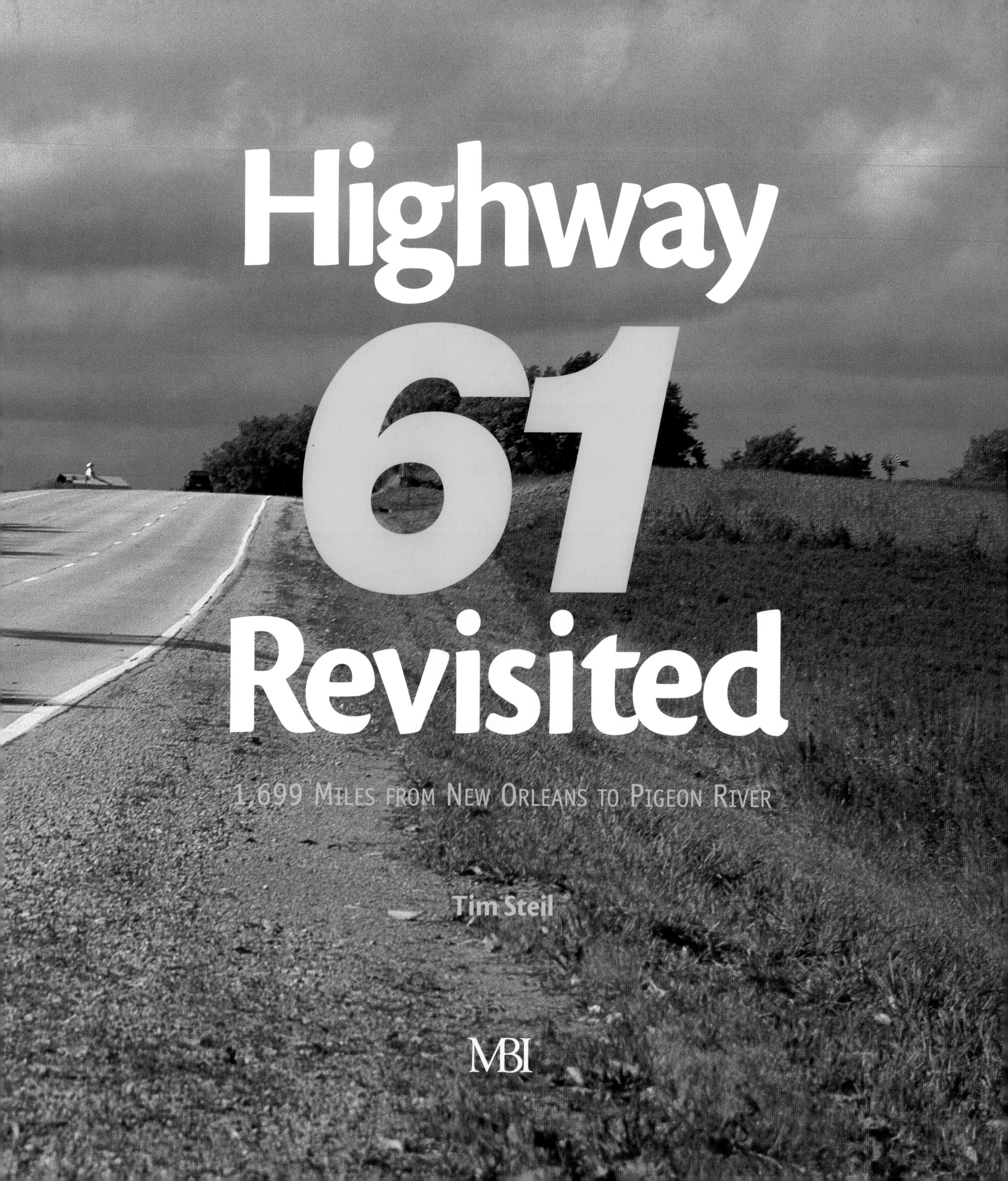

Highway
61
Revisited

1,699 MILES FROM NEW ORLEANS TO PIGEON RIVER

Tim Steil

MBI

This edition first published in 2004 by MBI Publishing Company, Galtier Plaza, Suite 200, 80 Jackson Street, St. Paul, MN 55101-3885 USA

MBI titles are also available at discounts in bulk quantity for industrial or sales-promotional use. For details write to Special Sales Manager at Motorbooks International Wholesalers & Distributors, Galtier Plaza, Suite 200, 380 Jackson Street, St. Paul, MN 55101-3885 USA.

ISBN# 0-7603-1451-9

Edited by Dennis Pernu
Designed by Mandy Iverson

Printed in China

Uncredited photos are those of the author.

On the frontispiece: *A Highway 61 sign—and a gathering storm—just south of Dickeyville, Wisconsin.*

On the title page: *A brief respite of sunshine between rain showers while pushing north on 61 toward La Crosse, Wisconsin.*

On the contents page, top: *A high water table that makes underground burials unadvisable led to the creation of New Orleans' "cities of the dead."* JIM LUNING

On the contents page, middle: *A deer-crossing sign warns motorists along a rolling stretch of Highway 61 in southern Iowa.*

On the contents page, bottom:
A breakwater protects boats harbored in Lake Superior, near the mouth of Minnesota's French River.

Right: *The lyrics to "Amos Moses" ("Now, Amos Moses was a Cajun/He lived by himself in the swamp") are never far from one's mind in the backwaters of Louisiana. This canal runs parallel to Highway 61 near Baton Rouge.*

61 CONTENTS

INTRODUCTION

One of five stern-wheel paddleboats still operating on the Mississippi, the Julia Belle Swain *steams up the river near Winona, Minnesota.* Courtesy Joan Collins Publicity

Officially, Highway 61 runs about 1,700 miles between New Orleans and the Canadian border, but I think I put around three times that many miles on my van while in the process of writing this.

I've sweated like a hog through the humid backwaters of Louisiana and awoken covered in an early snow on the bluffs overlooking Old Frontenac in Minnesota. I've sucked down ice-cold Colt .45s with the gentlemen down on Sunflower Avenue in Clarksdale, Mississippi, and sipped a restorative cup of tea with a pair of orthodox nuns in Grand Marais, Minnesota. Although I have essentially traveled straight through the center of the United States, it's as if I have been through a number of foreign countries.

There's New Orleans—our own Montreal in a way, half French, blissfully unaware it is actually part of the South, and more than happy to let one act like a drunken lout, as long as you are leaving a trail of twenties in your wake.

Then comes Mississippi, where the ghosts of the past continue to poison the good intentions of the present, and on through Memphis, home to Elvis, Al Green, and barbecue so sinfully good one feels obligated to drop down on one knee and thank Jesus (while asking Allah's forgiveness) for the very existence of pulled pork.

Along the road in Arkansas there is little more than rusting beer cans and the memory of better days past. Two of the greatest American artists, Mark Twain and Chuck Berry, plied their trades in Missouri before venturing off into our great wide open. Iowa and Wisconsin are tied to the river like a child on apron strings, and Minnesota is the "Land of 10,000 Lakes" and at least half that many pie stands and bait shops.

A million stories can be found along Highway 61, some so wonderfully kitschy and down home they seem to embody the very term *Americana*. But there are also others that show the human animal at its lowest, most sinful state and serve as painful reminders of our greatest

A rocky point juts out into Lake Superior, forming a small cove north of Duluth, Minnesota.

shame as a nation. For all the good and bad along the way, there is an odd continuity to the road.

The same path that escaped slaves followed on their way north to freedom was used by civil rights workers on their way south a hundred years later. Up on the Canadian border, where trappers lugged 90-pound bales of beaver pelts across the Grand Portage in 1700, modern-day hikers do much the same and call it "recreation." And in between, generations of Americans have built their homes and livelihoods along the Mississippi River, only to watch it rise and destroy both with maddening regularity.

Somewhere in that sense of continuity, there is comfort to be found—knowledge that, for better or worse, life goes on. While life can indeed be unfair, cruel even, it is still preferable to the alternative.

If you find yourself in Memphis and fail to buy a shirt from Mr. Bernard Lansky (below right), one-time haberdasher to Elvis Presley, you are passing up the opportunity of a lifetime. BERNARD J. LANSKY COLLECTION

> # "O Public Road . . .you express me better than I can express myself."
>
> —Walt Whitman

Other than that, there's not much by way of recommendation here. What follows is not a travel piece for some airline magazine or your Sunday newspaper insert. It is an honest reflection of what happened to me one summer on the road. It's a hell of a country, this United States of America, and I am grateful for both the opportunity to travel it and for the privilege of being able to share some of the things I've seen.

This is what I saw.

These are the things I did.

Fasten your seatbelt.

On the Lake Superior's North Shore, where trappers once lugged 90-pound bales of beaver pelts, modern-day hikers do much the same and call it "recreation." This trio is exploring near the Baptism River north of Duluth. MINNESOTA OFFICE OF TOURISM

61 Act I: New Orleans to Tunica

A lichen-covered statue greets those who come to pay their respects at a small cemetery in St. Francisville, Louisiana.

A snowy egret rests by the side of Highway 61 as the road winds north and west toward Baton Rouge. Despite the heavy industry in the area, it is still home to several varieties of migratory and native birds.

HIGHWAY 61:
The Other Mother Road

Highway 61, like its western cousin, Route 66, is what could safely be called a great American road. Along almost 2,000 miles between the Gulf of Mexico and the Canadian border, it connects not only towns and states, but also sweeping passages in our history as a people. And having traveled both from end to end over the years, I've noticed one important difference between the two roads.

Stop just about anywhere along Route 66 and, without fail, one of the first things folks will tell you is that you can get all the way to Los Angeles or Chicago by following the old road one way or the other. But while just as many people have heard of Highway 61 (thanks mostly to Mississippi Fred McDowell and Bob Dylan), even those who live along the road never seem to realize it runs the entire length of the country. They are acutely aware of their own state, or particular chunk of it, but when told the highway's actual terminal points, the fact comes back to them in either a slow, dawning recollection or a quizzical, "Really? Are you sure?"

Perhaps this is because The Mother Road has been known as just that ever since John Steinbeck used the phrase in *The Grapes of Wrath*, while Highway 61 has always been known by different names, depending where along the way you are. To add to the confusion, over the years the path of Highway 61 has become entwined with other roads so that some stretches are three different numbered highways at the same time.

Down in Mississippi it's "61 Highway," in southern Wisconsin they call it the "Trout Road," in Memphis it's "Second Street," and in St. Louis "Lindbergh Boulevard." Up north, long stretches are the "Great River Road." Down in New Orleans, on the edge of the French Quarter where Highway 61 and my travels began, it's "Tulane Avenue."

A panoramic view of the Louisiana state capitol building in Baton Rouge, circa 1909. The federal government commissioned similar bird's-eye views of many cities throughout the United States. LIBRARY OF CONGRESS

Long part of the traditional "jazz funeral," an impromptu marching band patrols the streets of the French Quarter. New Orleans is one of the few cities that tolerate strolling tuba players. During jazz festival weekends, heightened police patrols help guard against underground activity by pro-tuba radicals. JIM LUNING

Saturday Morning Coming Down

It is Saturday morning in the Big Easy, and this is not a good thing. Not that there is anything inherently wrong with New Orleans as a city, or Saturday as a day of the week, but when you put the two together, you invariably come up with something that follows Friday night in the Crescent City. Thus begins a tale of modified woe.

The lay of the land looks like this: several empty Jack Daniels bottles are strewn about the room, a large pointy-sideburned presence (later identified as a photographer) snores in the next bed, and the gnawed remains of room service past wafts stale Tabasco and alligator meat into the air. After a quick check for fresh tattoos and receipts from bail bondsmen—thankfully finding neither—I'm left to ponder which could be summoned faster: room service and a Bloody Mary or a priest to administer last rites. As it turns out, even in New Orleans, a city known for being open 24/7, priests simply do not deliver to hotel rooms.

If you are traveling with a wad of benjamins, sans a family or any sense of adult responsibility, New Orleans is less a place to visit than one to survive. The music tends to be too loud, and the cabs too rattletrap. The food runs spicy, and the cops are just crooked enough. And while the murder rate experiences some seasonal highs, mostly it's a damned fine town where a fellow needs to make a genuine effort to get himself arrested.

While I suppose some people come here to visit a museum or conduct legitimate business, more often than not, anyone rolling into this city will spend the bulk of their time doing one thing: drinking alcohol.

Every city has its own peculiar lifeblood, that essence which keeps its people and industry humming along in either outright or approximated prosperity. Out in Amarillo, it's helium; down in Albuquerque, weapons-grade plutonium. And way down yonder in New Orleans, it's fruit punch drink mix. Put it together with copious amounts of alcohol and a bit of ice, and it is possible to decant the very soul of the city into a 26-ounce glass. Umbrella optional.

Due to the high water table in the area, folks in New Orleans tend to bury their dead above ground. These burial vaults were immortalized (pun intended) in the movie Easy Rider. New Orleans Metropolitan Convention and Visitors Bureau. Photo by Ann Purcell

His bass player and accordionist missing in action, a street musician tunes his guitar between sets on Royal Street in the French Quarter. Jim Luning

The *Royal Café*, at the corner of Royal and St. Peter Streets, New Orleans. JIM LUNING

The *Hurricane,* named both for the shape of the glass it is served in and the swath of destruction often left in its path, is served all over New Orleans. Although the locals may turn their noses up at them, they have been popular in the tourist trade for years. Pat O'Briens, a suitable gin mill in the French Quarter, is famous for theirs, which according to a restaurant representative is made thusly:

> In a 26 oz. Hurricane glass,
> mix 4 oz. of Pat O'Brien's Hurricane Rum
> or a good dark rum
> and 4 oz. of Pat O'Brien's Hurricane Mix.
> Fill with crushed ice,
> and garnish with an orange slice and cherry.

The No. 904, also known as a streetcar named St. Charles, works the streets of New Orleans. JIM LUNING

But once you have had a couple of these cocktails in different parts of town, one's discerning palate will begin to consider the fact that occasionally the recipe is closer to this:

In a 26 oz. plastic cup,

mix one bottle 151 proof rum or grain alcohol

(kerosene may be used in a pinch).

Using an atomizer, add Hawaiian Punch

until liquid is tinted slightly,

fill with crushed ice, garnish with orange slice or cherry.

Secure customer to barstool using duct tape or staple gun.

Obtain payment or credit card number

before serving second drink.

The Hurricane, *named both for shape of the glass it is served in and the swath of destruction often left in its path.* New Orleans Metropolitan Convention and Visitors Bureau. Photo by Richard Nowitz

Whatever variety folks are sampling, they cart them around the Quarter *con brio*, often stopping in an alleyway to recycle them via one orifice or another, dodging cop-festooned horses, pickpockets, and hookers, and somehow making it back to their hotels and ultimately Omaha or Louisville or wherever.

This sign marks the junction of Highways 61 and 90, on the edge of New Orleans.

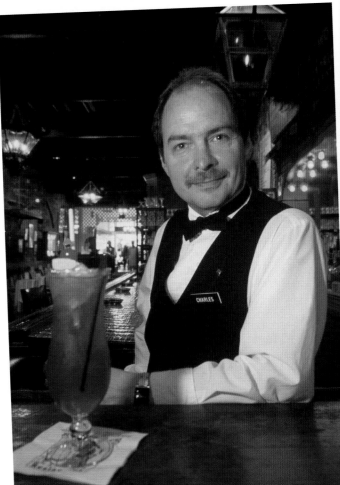

The Hackberry Ramblers: Now *That's* Old School

The Hackberry Ramblers' 1997 album, DEEP WATER, features guest appearances by Marcia Ball, Jimmie Dale Gilmore, and many others. After its release, critics around the world fumbled for new ways to say "incredible." HOT BISCUITS RECORDING COMPANY. PHOTO BY RICK OLIVIER

Louisiana has always been famous for its vibrant music scene. From the classic Dixieland at Preservation Hall, to the fried okra funk of the Meters and Dr. John, the region has spawned a diverse group of players whose influence can be heard in the top-ten records of just about any decade. While the biggest act to come out of Louisiana these days is an ex-Mouseketeer with fake tits and voice courtesy of Pro-Tools, the true sounds of the Pelican State have been echoing out of the bayou since the 1930s.

Whether it is because of the sheer length of their career or the grizzled catcher's mitt that Keith Richards' face has become, somewhere along the line the Rolling Stones got dubbed "the world's oldest rock n' roll band." Although now over 60, Mick Jagger can still prance about the stage like he was a mere kid of say, 45, but it is doubtful he and the rest of the boys will be doing much more than counting their royalties in 30 years.

During the time the Stones began plunking out old blues and Chuck Berry covers in London dives, the Hackberry Ramblers had already been rocking the bayou for three decades.

Cajun music is played predominantly on the button, or accordion. Unlike its cousin, the piano accordion, the button model produces a different note, depending on whether the bellows are pumped or pulled.

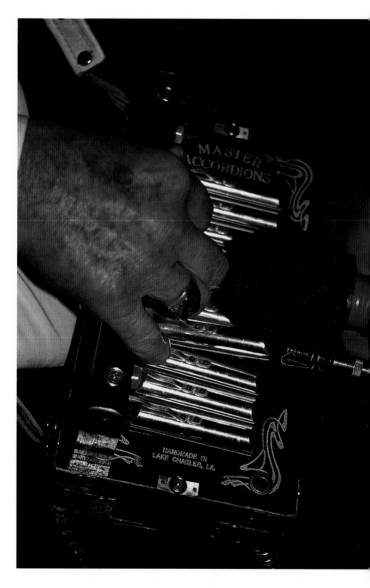

Luderin Darbone, the nonagenarian founder and fiddler of the Hackberry Ramblers, kicks off a song for a receptive crowd. Whether you're just off the boat or straight outta Compton, when you come to a Hackberry Ramblers show, you're a Cajun. And you dance.

In 1933, fiddler Luderin Darbone and his accordion-playing friend, Ed Duhon, began playing dancehalls and house parties in western Louisiana. Back then many of the places didn't have proper electricity, so they used a handcrafted transformer to run their amplifiers off the battery of Darbone's Model-T, which they would leave idling behind the building.

By 1935, they were so popular that they were signed to a recording contract with RCA's Bluebird subsidiary. They enjoyed great regional hits with "Wondering, Wondering," and the Cajun classic "Jolie Blonde." They continued playing and recording until the 1960s. Then rock n' roll took the country by storm, making just about everything else sound dated.

But at the same time, a renewed interest in authentic folk music began reviving the careers of aging blues singers, and the Ramblers saw their stock rise again. Beginning in 1963, they started recording for Arhoolie Records, which also re-released some of their original recordings from the 1930s.

In 1970, thanks to a hand-me-down album from my brother Greg, I met The Night Tripper, a Voodoo Priest from New Orleans who went by the name "Dr. John" during daylight hours. In 1988, while I was doing shots of cognac with Junior Wells backstage at the Chicago Blues Festival, this guy named Mac Rebenac shuffled into the tent. He said, "Howdy." We said, "Howdy" back.
COURTESY ATLANTIC RECORDS

For the next 20 years they soldiered along, playing sporadically. In the 1980s, when MTV turned the music industry into a style-over-substance affair, an equal and opposite reaction occurred: another revival of interest in American roots music. By then, the Ramblers were not simply a regional oddity, but bona fide legends.

One can only imagine what was going through the boys' heads when they performed at the Super Bowl in 1996 or their thoughts when they get booked to play music festivals in France, where they are treated like royalty. Beyond the ups and downs of a career spanning 70 years, the one constant has always been the music.

✦ ✦ ✦

As the Ramblers take the stage in their trademark white shirts, red suspenders, and cowboy hats, Ed Duhon squeezes a few chords out of his button accordion as Luderin Darbone fiddles with the knobs on his amplifier, occasionally sawing a double stop to check his tone. Then they're off.

Though rooted in the Cajun sounds of western Louisiana, the Ramblers serve up a stew of traditional ballads ("Frankie and Johnny"), western swing ("Deep Water"), and even once-great-but-now-passé rock standards ("Proud Mary"). But whatever they do play, they make it rock. Darbone's fiddle recalls the ragged but right greasiness of Gid Tanner and the Skillet Lickers, and when Duhon leans into his squeeze box to kick off songs such as "Poor Hobo" or "J'étais au Bal Hier Soir," it's rousing enough to wake the dead.

There's no one in the band younger than 50, but once on stage the years fall away, and they become the world's greatest party band, whooping and hollering, singing in French one minute, English the next, and driving the crowd into a frenzy. And whether you're from Boston or Phoenix or Calcutta, you're a Cajun by the time the set is over.

Edwin Duhon, accordionist and cofounder of the Hackberry Ramblers, relaxes backstage before a show at a New Orleans music festival. After Ramblers' shows, he can typically be found chatting up the local talent, who find him irresistible.

Sam's Place: Funk Palace Supreme

After having dinner in the French Quarter, I got back to the hotel room late and realized that the tobacco supply was on the wane, so I went back downstairs and tried the bar to no avail. I checked at the front desk, and they informed me that the nearest place to get a pack of smokes at that hour was a gas station down the street. Stepping outside, I looked in the direction the clerk had pointed and saw, perhaps ten blocks away, a tiny gas station sign.

With the late hour and all, I didn't much feel like walking all that way, and I was too lazy to get the car out of the garage and too cheap to spring for a cab. I walked around the corner looking for signs of life and ran into a fellow waiting at a bus stop.

"You know where I can cop a pack of smokes around here?" I asked.

"Oh . . . yeah, man," he smiled. "Just git up in this little club around the corner. They'll take care of you."

"They have a cigarette machine?" I asked, just to double check.

"Man, they got everything. Go on now. There ain't no sign or nothing, but you'll see it. Go on now, man," he assured me.

I walked around the corner and, about halfway down the block, spotted an opaque door held open just

Urging dancers onto the floor with a quick wit and mix skills, a DJ keeps the music flowing on Sam's opening night.

Inside the club, old-school funk and stepping music rule the evening. Unlike a club down the street, no rap music is played at Sam's.

Your proprietor, Sam, with a friend outside Sam's Place on Tulane Avenue in New Orleans.

a crack by a brick. As the guy had said, there was no sign, but I could hear some really fine music and voices coming from inside. I figured it must be the place.

I stepped inside and immediately noticed a largish sign that read:

**25 and older only
NO bandanas allowed
NO rap music played**

It was like that rather comical scene from the movie *Animal House*, where the Delta house lads decide to go see Otis Day and the Knights on the band's home turf. There was a DJ in the far corner pumping out old-school funk and about 75 people around the bar and out on the dance floor. They had two things in common: they were all the same race, and they all looked at me like I had two heads.

I stepped up to the bar and politely asked for change for the cigarette machine and was about to start sliding

A stunning night scene in the French Quarter. NEW ORLEANS METROPOLITAN CONVENTION AND VISITORS BUREAU. PHOTO BY RICHARD NOWITZ

dollars into the thing when one of the fellows at the bar jumped next to me and said, "Hold up now!"

He warned me that the machine was unplugged, and I was about to lose my money. I waited as he and another fellow found an extension cord to plug it back in. There was only one small problem—it was the power supply to the DJ's sound system.

There are awkward silences, there are *damned* awkward silences, and then there was this. The crowd waited while they shut down the music and I got my pack of cigarettes and things got back to normal. Figuring I had made enough of a first impression for one evening, I thanked the fellow who plugged in the machine and quickly cut out.

The next night, after another dinner in a different part of town, I found myself back at the hotel in the same situation when a light bulb when on. "What the hell," I thought, as I stepped out onto the street and headed back for the little club. It was still early, I was bored, and I figured even if I ended up getting launched

into the street by unappreciative customers, it would be worth writing about.

Coming from the other direction this time, I noticed a handwritten sign in the window that said, "Sam's Place—Opening Weekend!" Once inside I noticed a few familiar faces, including the fellow who hooked up the butt vendor for me the night before. I found a seat at the bar and ordered a beer. The prices were a little steep, but then again, this was New Orleans, and the fine spread of free eats laid out at the end of the bar more than made up for it.

The DJ, the same as the night before, kept up a steady stream of the same old-school funk I grew up on and that you just don't hear anymore, unless you're a stepper from the South Side of Chicago or you find yourself in a place like, well, a place like this. There was Sly and the Family Stone, Al Green, The Dramatics, Roy Ayers, Lonnie Liston-Smith, and more. But when I heard the opening notes of Lakeside's "Fantastic Voyage," I knew I had come as close to heaven as I dare hope to find that night. I decided then and there that if anyone was going to try

A glimpse of old neon is visible on the Art Deco façade of Airline Motors, an old car dealership on the Airline Highway—aka Highway 61—on the way out of New Orleans. JIM LUNING

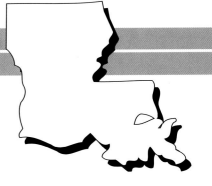

to bounce my ass out the door, that person would have to be pretty damned convincing or pretty damned big—probably both.

About an hour later, I was talking with a guy who was, like myself, a former military aviator. We were standing in a corner swapping war stories when I felt a hand clap me on the shoulder and the voice of Barry White ask, "So you enjoying yourself here, man?"

As I turned around, I saw he was an inch or two shorter than me (I'm 6-foot-6) and had muscles in the places I had bones.

"Uh…just got here, man," I answered, unsure of what exactly was going on.

He took my elbow, walked me up to the bar, and called the bartender.

"You get this man anything he wants," he told her. "On me."

When I turned around to thank him he already had his hand out and grabbed mine, shaking it.

"I'm Sam, man. Welcome to my place," he said with a smile.

As I would come to learn, there was a rather large and boisterous place just down the street that catered to a younger crowd, where rap music was indeed played, and the clientele wore or carried bandanas that had nothing to do with the ranches on which they were herding cattle. Sam had opened his place to give the more mature

crowd somewhere to come without worrying about gang shootings and hear music that spoke to the positive side of life, not the darkness that had enveloped so much of his community over the last decade.

I came for the music. I came for the beer. But mostly I came because I was bored and I figured regardless of what happened, it would be a worthwhile experience. I had no idea what I would find, other than perhaps a DJ who would give me the stink-eye for blowing his flow the night before.

I ended up having one of the most memorable nights of my life, full of friendship, with a soundtrack that could have been pulled from my own record collection. Although the details tend to get fuzzier the later the night got, I am pretty sure I was dancing before I left and stumbled back to my hotel. Just to put it in perspective, the only times yours truly dances is if I have just said, "I do" or someone is shooting at my feet. It was that good.

The next morning I departed for Mississippi with a splitting headache, a photographer, and a vague but certain knowledge that there are things that bind us, no matter how divergent our backgrounds may be. If only those experiences were as easy for the rest of the world to find as they were for me that night. A Lakeside record and a beer—could it really be that simple?

The greater Baton Rouge area is home to numerous refineries and processing facilities, like this ExxonMobil chemical plant south of town. Jim Luning

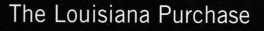

The Myrtles Plantation: A Haunted History?

It is known, at least among those who track such things, as one of the most haunted places in the South. Although there are the true believers and the dyed-in-the-wool skeptics, when it comes to ghosts and paranormal activity, most at least entertain such claims if the case seems strong enough. The legend wrapped around the Myrtles Plantation is a juicy one, indeed, equal parts Southern gothic and *The Ghost and Mr. Chicken*.

This much we know. General David Bradford was a wealthy judge and businessman from Pennsylvania who served under George Washington. He had been interested in the land around what would become St. Francisville for some time before he had the dumb luck of plotting against Washington in the ill-fated Whiskey Rebellion of 1794. He fled from from the north that year, and received a land grant of 650 acres from the Spanish.

Bradford built the plantation that would come to be known as the Myrtles in 1797, and when he died nine years later, his wife sold the property to their son-in-law, a lawyer friend of Andrew Jackson. In 1834, the property passed to the family of Ruffin Stirling, who lived in the house for the next 60 years, restoring it along the way. After that, the house changed ownership several times before a proper restoration began in the early 1970s. But it is Bradford's family that has had the greatest influence on the place, and the story surrounding his daughter's death that has given it its claim to fame.

The Myrtles Plantation, either the most haunted or most hyped attraction in the St. Francisville area. Though it claims a murderous past, some historians claim most of the deaths there were due to yellow fever, not foul play. JIM LUNING

The Louisiana Purchase

The French first built a fort in this part of what is now Louisiana in 1729 and, as the French are wont to do on occasion, promptly abandoned it. For the next 80-odd years, the surrounding area was passed back and forth between France, Spain, and England, but its residents always retained a fiercely independent spirit. George Washington's fledgling administration began working out the terms of what would become the Louisiana Purchase in 1795, but it wasn't until eight years later that anything came to fruition. When President Thomas Jefferson learned that the Spanish had secretly ceded the area back to France, he sent an emissary to negotiate for outright possession of New Orleans or, at the least, guaranteed trading rights in that crucial port. By December 1802, they were at a stalemate.

In January 1803, Jefferson sent future president James Monroe to France with $2 million and orders to secure New Orleans, authorizing Monroe to offer up to $10 million. In the end, Monroe promised the French $15 million, but secured lands far in excess of what Jefferson had ordered. For roughly four cents an acre, he bought up 828,000 square miles of virgin country, doubling the size of the nation. Yet, for the settlers in what would become St. Francisville, there was one regrettable detail. The eastern border of the Louisiana Purchase was the Mississippi River, just a few miles to the west, and so they remained part of Spanish-held West Florida.

In 1804, the United States set up a territorial government in the new land and by 1812 had carved Louisiana, the first of 13 states, out of the purchase.

Clark Woodruffe was married to General Bradford's daughter, Sara. Although a respected man in his community, he, as was the wont of many plantation owners, was in the habit of having sex with one of the female house slaves, in this case a girl named Chloe. (Though common at the time, these sorts of master-slave relationships amounted to nothing less than rape.)

When Woodruffe grew tired of Chloe and picked a new slave as the object of his unsavory attentions, Chloe became worried that she would be sent to the fields to work and often eavesdropped on family conversations, hoping her name would not come up. When Woodruffe discovered this, he had one of her ears cut off as punishment.

Now wearing a turban to cover her wound, Chloe came up with a plan she thought would regain Woodruffe's favor. She poisoned his oldest daughter's birthday cake, thinking that the dedication she would consequently display in nursing the family back to health would keep her from being sent to the field. But she put too much poison in the cake and killed her master's wife and two daughters, as well as his unborn third child. The other slaves, fearing the master's rage would be visited on them as well, hung Chloe from a tree on the grounds, then cut down her lifeless body and tossed it into a nearby river. Since then, the ghost of Chloe has been haunting the place, as have those of the Woodruffe children, who can reportedly be heard playing outside.

This story has become part of the canon of the place, passed along for decades among paranormal researchers and amateur ghost hounds. More than one local historian believes the story is pure hokum, and that, with the exception of one verified murder on the plantation around the time of the Civil War, everyone who died there expired from either natural causes or yellow fever. Regardless, the story endures, and each year hundreds of visitors come, hoping to catch a glimpse of Chloe or some other small bit of weirdness.

✦　✦　✦

In the course of researching this book, I sent out many queries about the validity of the legend or experiences people might have had there. Many folks wrote back, claiming to have seen things that were "beyond belief," or swearing that the entire St. Francisville area is haunted. As one person noted, "The vibes there are just tuned higher."

There were reports of organs playing and glasses tinkling in the middle of the night, pictures with eyes that follow you, ghostly reflections in mirrors, and, of course, the ever-popular ghosts of Chloe hanging in a tree and the Woodruffe children playing outside.

Keeping the Mississippi River navigable means constant dredging of the silt that washes into Louisiana all the way from northern Minnesota. This new barge is working the river just north of St. Francisville. JIM LUNING

Magnificent plantations, some fully restored, line Highway 61 as it rolls north out of St. Francisville, Louisiana. Of course, Newton's First Law of Physics is also in effect, as evidenced by these rundown shacks across 61. JIM LUNING

None of the people I corresponded with seemed especially loopy in their tone, but they all did seem to have visited the place expecting ghosts, and were therefore more accepting of the notion in the first place. And while I was rather skeptical of the whole thing in the beginning, in reflection it seems an innocent, almost benevolent preoccupation.

People walk into tent revivals expecting to be cured, and sometimes, inexplicably, they are. Others walk into a casino expecting to get rich, and sometimes, against incredible odds, they do. Doctors have prescribed placebos for almost 200 years, assuming that the power of the human mind can accomplish things that hard science has no way to explain. And sometimes it does.

In the end, I suppose that if you believe in ghosts and go the Myrtles Plantation looking for them, you will indeed encounter them. But if your tastes in tales of pure horror lean more toward the true, then you just need to drive a little farther, friend. A little farther.

A sign over the roadway welcomes travelers getting off the St. Francisville ferry a few miles west of town. West Feliciana Parish actually declared itself the Republic of West Florida in the early 1800s after being left out of the Lousiana Purchase. The United States annexed the parish a few months later.

Plantation Row

Today, as you head north out of St. Francisville, Louisiana, along Highway 61 you encounter something of a Plantation Row. There are fine old antebellum houses, brimming with tour groups and surrounded by splendid gardens. Then there are old shotgun shacks, where the less fortunate spend their lives. You can almost hear the swarms of flies that populate them in the summer and the icy winds that whistle through them in the winter.

Ironically, it seems hard times are harder on the folks in the "big house," as they're called. They have the unenviable job of keeping up these old buildings, and since the plantation system no longer has a steady supply of slave labor, they have to look elsewhere for a cash flow when times get lean.

Most of these places have embraced the tourist industry, becoming bed-and-breakfasts or simply offering tours of their grounds and homes. If they are lucky, there is some distinct angle they can play up to distinguish themselves from their neighbors.

One of the many such plantations along the way, built by a former Continental Army general who went on to try to overthrow the fledgling colonial government, claims to be full of ghosts.

Statuary populates a cemetery behind a church in St. Francisville.

Anne Butler and the Butler Greenwood Plantation

As you pull off Highway 61 and down the winding gravel lane that leads to Butler Greenwood Plantation, Spanish moss waves lazily in the scant summer breeze. The live oaks that line the roadway were planted in 1790 and their acorns became the mighty oaks growing on the grounds of Grace Church back in town.

Nearing the main house of Butler Greenwood, with its light purple exterior and row of rocking chairs aligned in front, is like stepping back in time. The grounds cover some 50 acres, with a duck pond, a swimming pool, gardens, and winding trails leading in and around the lot of them.

There is a touch of the Southern belle in Anne Butler, but it's not a floppy hat and parasol that she calls to mind as much as the shotgun over the hearth. To say she has a cast-iron will would be faint praise. To suggest that she wasn't born into this land and this house as much as she was mined and forged like steel would be more accurate. In fact, having just now compared her to a Southern belle, I fear on our next meeting, Anne Butler might just give me a well-deserved elbow in the ribs for suggesting such ridiculousness.

✦ ✦ ✦

It was Sunday morning in 1997, and after attending services at Grace and shepherding a group of visiting travel agents about the grounds of Butler Greenwood,

Anne Butler: journalist, author, survivor. Her family first came to the St. Francisville area in the 1790s. Her ancestors served in the army with both George Washington and Andrew Jackson. JIM LUNING

Anne Butler was having coffee with her husband on the back porch. The glorious late summer morning and idyllic setting did nothing to allay the tension in the air that day.

Butler had been married to Murray Henderson for seven years. It was an unconventional arrangement from the start. The two met while collaborating on a book, she an experienced journalist, and he a respected criminologist much her senior. A relationship ensued, and when the book was finally completed and the smoke cleared, Henderson left his wife of 40 years, Butler left her husband, and the new couple set up household at Butler Greenwood.

In hindsight, Butler says she could see the writing on the wall almost immediately. Henderson never seemed to fit into the place and became resentful and jealous of the love and attention she paid to her ancestral home. Over the years they separated many times, always returning to the familiar, if uncomfortable life they had made together.

And so it went this lazy summer morning. Gone for a week, Henderson had inevitably returned to the plantation, and Butler wasn't surprised to see him. She calmly fixed him a cup of coffee and settled into a chair on the porch for what she assumed would be the same conversation they had had several times before.

Then Murray Henderson stood up, took a black .38 caliber pistol out of his pocket, and pulled the trigger.

The rocker-lined front porch at Butler Greenwood provides shady release from the relentless southern sun. Guests often relax there after dinner, and groups bide their time until the next tour.

The oaks that line the winding gravel lane to Butler Greenwood Plantation are very much alive and more than 200 years old.

✦ ✦ ✦

The plantation was established in the late 1700s, when Anne Butler's ancestors arrived by wagon from Pennsylvania and set up a household near Bayou Sara. While many settlers arrived in the area with not much more than the clothes on their backs and good intentions, Butler's people built a respectable English cottage with a well-appointed library and a music room featuring both a concert grand piano and a gilded harp.

Five of the Butler brothers served on the staff of George Washington during the American Revolution. A decade and a half later, more served Andrew Jackson at the Battle of New Orleans. They were well educated, equally cultured, and as independent as they came. There was always something of a class distinction between the French and English settlers in the region, both sides assuming something superior about their own roots. It was into this proud history and love of tradition that Anne Butler was born in 1944.

Though her parents lived just down the road in Baton Rouge, she spent many childhood summers and weekends on the plantation, visiting her grandmother and great-aunt, swimming with a gaggle of cousins, and soaking up the history of her family and the region.

When Anne Butler decided to turn her ancestral home into a bed and breakfast, she updated many of the buildings, installed a pool, and added this gazebo. Courtesy Butler Greenwood Plantation

The table in Butler Greenwood's airy dining room is set with period china. The design of the house does not feature hallways, which keeps a cooling breeze flowing from room to room. Courtesy Butler Greenwood Plantation

Butler Greenwood's interior has been carefully preserved and, according to state preservation officials, is one of the most important historical buildings in Louisiana. Courtesy Butler Greenwood Plantation

After receiving a bachelor's degree from Sweet Briar College, she switched coasts and completed her graduate work in California, receiving a master's degree in English from Humboldt State. Although, like many young people in the late 1960s, she felt a bit of disdain for the establishment and the old plantation's representation of it, she returned to St. Francisville in 1970 and never left again.

Over the years, she restored the old house and built guest cottages in back, turning the place into one of the area's most popular bed-and-breakfasts. The house's stunning period interior and manicured grounds are also popular with the many day tours operating in the area, which she accommodates during normal business hours.

And if that wasn't enough to keep her busy, Anne Butler also found time to write 10 books, everything from local histories and tourist guides, to a book about Angola State Penitentiary just a few miles away. Her co-author on that one was Murray Henderson, who knew the place well. He was the former warden.

One summer morning, Anne Butler's husband stood up, pulled a pistol from his pocket, and began firing. The harrowing story of that day and its aftermath is told in Weep for the Living, *a book Butler began to work on as soon as she was able to sit at a desk again.* Courtesy Anne Butler

✦ ✦ ✦

The first bullet tore into Butler's abdomen, and as she swung forward in her chair trying to rise, Henderson quickly fired three more times, striking her kidney, rupturing her intestines, and barely missing her spinal cord. Knocked back into her chair and bleeding profusely, there was little she could do but watch as he fired two more shots, one bullet lodging in her shoulder, the other shattering her right elbow. Then Murray Henderson, a recovering alcoholic, strolled into the next room and began chugging vermouth straight from the bottle. Then he reloaded his gun. It was sometime between 10:30 and 11:00 A.M.

When she realized Henderson was going to sit there and watch her die, Butler decided to play possum. She slumped to one side and breathed as shallowly as possible, taking deep breaths when Henderson looked away or momentarily left the room. Although her fate seemed sealed, there was a remote chance for survival.

The maids arrived just before noon to clean the cottages and do laundry. When one approached the porch door, loaded down with laundry, Butler appeared to be sleeping. The maid, while a valued employee, was not known much for her powers of observation. She walked within a foot of Butler twice, but failed to notice that her boss was bleeding to death. She later told the police she *did* think it was odd that Butler had been napping that early and also wondered why she had changed into a red sweater.

The other maid arrived shortly after the first and immediately realized what was going on. When she screamed that Butler needed a doctor, Henderson told the maid that Butler was already gone and to go away as it didn't concern her. Backing away from the door carefully, she immediately went to a pay phone and called for help. The news flew around West Feliciana Parish.

It was after one o'clock when that call was made to 911, and by then help was barreling toward the plantation. Butler's eyes were open just a slit, but she could make out the figure of a sheriff's deputy creeping up the back walk when another flew through the door and grabbed her by the legs, pulling her to safety.

When they saw Henderson in the kitchen, reaching into his pocket, both officers screamed at him to drop the gun, but he refused. When they tackled him, one of the deputies grabbed his hand to keep the barrel of the revolver from spinning. Even as they disarmed him, Henderson's finger was on the trigger, pulling it fruitlessly.

As the paramedics arrived and loaded Butler in the back of an ambulance for the 20-mile drive to the nearest hospital, the chief deputy on the scene informed the family there was no way Butler would survive her wounds and that they should start making funeral arrangements.

Henderson, other than protesting his rough treatment at the hands of the police, didn't say much of anything. He was well connected in the area, and almost immediately that influence was obvious. He was charged with attempted second-degree murder and out on bail in less than 24 hours.

What followed for Butler must have been worse than the shooting itself. Once released from intensive care, she was deluged with meetings with detectives and attorneys and visits from well-wishing family and friends. Massive surgery was followed by strict regimens of painful physical therapy, then more surgeries, a half-dozen procedures in all. But it wasn't merely physical pain that would torment her.

As she recovered from her wounds, Butler had both Henderson's criminal trial and their divorce proceedings to deal with. Of course, she also had a business to run, and her insurance was running out. Through the dedication of many family and friends, Butler managed to keep the plantation afloat, get a divorce, and see Murray Henderson sent to jail.

As soon as she was recovered enough to sit up at a computer, Anne Butler began pecking out notes and ideas for what would become *Weep for the Living*, her book that recounts the shooting and its maddening aftermath. It's a veritable primer on law and order that also covers much of the history of West Feliciana Parish.

It, like many of Butler's other books, are for sale in the gift shop at Butler Greenwood, and between checking guests in and out and dealing with the laundry and garden and tours, which come often enough to be a chore, she sells a few. Once the guests are safely ensconced and the tours are through, Butler is left to an evening's peace in a place that has been a spiritual home for more than 200 years.

These old stone steps, Spanish moss hanging overhead, lead down one of the many garden paths on the grounds of Butler Greenwood. The entire region is renowned for its plantation gardens.

You in Mississippi Now, Boy

If changes in American society—be they progressive politics or the use of avocados on a perfectly good cheeseburger—tend to start out in New York or Los Angeles, there is little doubt about where change arrives last, and with the most difficulty.

Mississippi.

Though things have indeed changed for the better since the advent of the civil rights movement, there is still a tacit uneasiness about the place, and it lingers in the air like the ozone after a lightning strike. It is a place that remains chained to its painful past, even as it tries to distance itself from it. Although they do not speak of it openly—or much at all, for that matter—there are still people here who remember the old ways. Fondly.

For every Elvis Presley, there is an Emmett Till, and for every Hodding Carter, a Sam Bowers. All over the state there are stark reminders of what was, what the future could hold, and the things that will never be.

As you roll into the south end of Natchez, you encounter Mammy's Café, a certified roadside attraction for several reasons, including its unique architecture, its

folksy charm, and the outright offense it still presents to a good portion of the people who see it.

Sambo's Restaurants took down their signs almost two decades ago and rebranded themselves something more palatable. Of course, here in Mississippi at that time, they had yet to get around to removing all the "Whites Only" signs from drinking fountains.

There are symbols, and then there are metaphors. Then there is the place we are headed next. If ever there was a sight that encompassed the moth-eaten carcass of the Confederacy, it is just off Highway 61 between Natchez and Vicksburg.

> *"Have anything changed?*
> *Have anything changed?!*
> *Go take a look around, boy.*
> *You tell me."*
>
> — *A black Mississippian who asked to remain nameless*

An old general store sits along Highway 61 as the road pushes north toward the Mississippi border. The first and only road-kill chicken of the trip was encountered just up the road. JIM LUNING

This abandoned juke joint, complete with a Jax Beer sign and corrugated tin roof, sits just over the border from Louisiana. JIM LUNING

Mammy's Café, a historic if questionable piece of roadside architecture just south of Natchez, Mississippi, welcomes travelers on Highway 61 North. Mammy's is open mostly for breakfast and lunch and sells homemade jams and baked goods. JIM LUNING

A small restaurant and bar in the area known as Natchez Under the Hill, an old riverfront strip known for its taverns, brothels, and fights. JIM LUNING

The Ruins of Windsor

Once the finest plantation in the South, Windsor is now a charred hulk, felled by a dropped cigar at the turn of the century. Even the railing that keeps visitors away from the crumbling columns, are made from charred wood, making the fire seem that much more recent. A closer look at the columns shows their remaining bits of wrought iron and ornately carved capitals, now favorite spots for nesting birds. JIM LUNING

Windsor Plantation does not want to be found, and I will not tell you how to find it here. There are enough historical records, enough guidebooks, and, these days, enough websites that will give you directions. Most of them are wrong. I followed several of them, and they sent me up the Natchez Trace dozens of miles in the wrong direction—a matter of East versus West, or perhaps more succinctly, North versus South.

Windsor is under siege these days. Not from the Union Army as it once was, but from the fields of kudzu that have swallowed much of the South with startling quickness. When General Ulysses S. Grant passed through this area on his way to Vicksburg, he looked at Port Gibson, today the town nearest to Windsor on Highway 61, and declared it was "too beautiful to burn."

There are no pictures of Windsor Plantation in its heyday. There is only a drawing taken from the notebook of a Union soldier, who was treated there when it was converted to a Union hospital during the "War between Brothers," or as it is know in these parts, "The War of Northern Aggression."

It is said that after the war, a cub steamboat pilot by the name of Samuel Clemens used Windsor as a navigation aid as he wound south toward Natchez and, ultimately, New Orleans.

This Natchez city park, complete with its requisite gazebo, sits atop a hill overlooking the Mississippi. JIM LUNING

Eudora Welty, the great writer and photographer who was able to decant the soul of Mississippi into words and paragraphs, came across this place once in the early 1940s. In her 1944 essay, "Some Notes on River Country," Welty wrote:

Winding through this land unwarned, rounding to a valley, you will come on a startling thing. Set back in an old gray field, with horses grazing like small fairy animals beside it, is a vast ruin—twenty-two Corinthian columns in an empty oblong and L. Almost seeming to float like lace, bits of wrought-iron balcony connect the here and there. Live cedar trees are growing from the iron black acanthus leaves, high in the empty air. This is the Ruin of Windsor, long since burned.

Throughout her essay, Welty describes this backcountry with love and precision. And it seems little has changed since she visited it almost 70 years ago. As I headed down this road to nowhere, huge pods of bagworms dangled from the overhanging branches. A few miles out of Port Gibson, a recently downed tree laid across the road, blocking it. A semi waited on the other side, its driver pacing and smoking alongside the truck and talking, agitated, into a cellular phone.

There was a small muddy bank on the roadside. I made it over, sliding this way and that, one ill-advised acceleration away from being mired to the lug nuts. The road continued—half blacktop, half good intentions—until I rounded the valley Welty described.

Then I saw the kudzu.

It is beautiful, yet chilling to behold. The rampant vine, once touted as a viable crop and a curative, can swamp a field in one season. It is a terror to the southern states, almost impossible to get rid of, and chokes the life out of everything it covers.

A small wooden sign, put up by the Mississippi Department of Something or Another, pointed me down the narrow gravel lane to the ruins themselves. It was drizzling rain, and I was surprised to see someone else already here, a black couple from Arizona, of all places, according to their license plates.

We exchanged silent waves and nods. The only sounds were the squealing of the birds that had nested in the tops of the columns and the steady patter of rain against the leaves.

Kudzu vine, originally imported from Japan as a soil stabilizer, animal food, and decorative vine, is choking Mississippi. It covers and destroys native species, growing up to 18 inches a day. Experts believe it takes 10 years of repeated burning and herbicide to remove a single stand. JIM LUNING

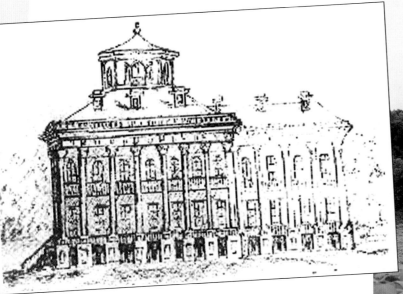

The only known image of Windsor Plantation in its heyday was taken from the notebook of a Union soldier who was treated there when it was used as a hospital during the Civil War. LIBRARY OF CONGRESS

The Siege of Vicksburg

In early April 1861, Ulysses S. Grant was living quietly in Galena, Illinois, and working with his brothers in the family leather goods store. A retired army officer and West Point graduate, he had served in the Mexican-American War and commanded units in Panama. When Abraham Lincoln called up the militias after the Confederate attack on Fort Sumter, Grant agreed to drill recruits in Galena but declined to become their captain.

But just over a month later, after watching Union troops attack a Confederate militia in St. Louis, he applied for a commission as a colonel and was eventually given command of the 21st Illinois Volunteers.

Over the next two years, he was promoted, then relieved of command and chastised by newspapers and fellow commanders alike for his bloody defeat at Shiloh. But regardless of his stormy relationships with superiors, he had one redeeming quality that the president noticed.

"This man," Lincoln said, "he fights."

♦　　♦　　♦

Vicksburg was an important control point along the lower Mississippi, and Grant had been trying to take the city since October 1862. He had fought numerous battles, even devised a plan to dig a canal, all to no avail.

On April 6, 1863, General Sherman—later famous for his march through Georgia—ordered Grant to bring his men back to Memphis and approach the city along the railroad lines. In defiance, Grant marched his troops south along the western edge of the river a few days later and had Admiral David Porter run his fleet past the batteries. By early May, with his armies in place near Grand Gulf, Grant was ready for a fresh assault on Vicksburg.

With two days' rations, he took his men into open country, away from his normal lines of communication.

An artist's depiction of the Siege of Vicksburg. LIBRARY OF CONGRESS

Ulysses S. Grant tried for months to take Vicksburg, but to no avail. Finally, after two last assaults on the city were repelled, he vowed to lay siege to it and either bomb or starve its citizenry to death. With their supply lines cut off, Confederate soldiers survived by eating their mules. LIBRARY OF CONGRESS

SIEGE OF VICKSBURG

> *"I now determined upon a regular siege—to 'out camp the enemy,' as it were, and incur no more losses."*
>
> — *Ulysses S. Grant, May 22, 1863*

In the next 20 days, he marched his troops over 200 miles, forced the evacuation of Grand Gulf, captured the capital, Jackson, and beat back two armies in five different battles. His troops killed over 6,000 rebels, took 6,500 prisoners, and destroyed more than 30 miles of railroad. On May 19, Grant was on the outskirts of Vicksburg; he assumed the Confederates would not put up much resistance. He was wrong.

On two separate attacks, the Confederate Army, dug into trenches, repulsed Grant's men. On May 22, he decided to lay siege to the city, slowly squeezing out the supplies of food and ammunition.

Over the next six weeks, things went downhill for both the Confederate soldiers and for Vicksburg's citizens. Under constant bombardment by Union artillery, there was hardly a building in town that didn't bear a scar. The men on the front lines were cut first to half, then quarter rations. Flour was selling for $5 a pound or $1,000 a barrel. Molasses was $12 a gallon. Beef—usually animals killed by shelling—was $2.50 a pound, and mule meat was $1 a pound. With all their fodder gone, the remaining horses were given corn silage.

By July 1, Grant's men had dug themselves within shouting distance of the enemy lines and the men from the opposing armies often yelled to each other. Grant decided they would make a final assault on the weakened city on July 6.

But on July 3, he received a message from the Confederate commander, General John Pemberton, proposing surrender and asking only that his men be able to keep their guns. Grant refused, saying any surrender

A view from the bluffs at the Vicksburg National Military Park. Its winding road is best driven slow, as it winds first through Union, then Confederate positions, before continuing on to the place most soldiers ended the conflict—the graveyards. JIM LUNING

A Confederate artillery installation, on the low ground at Vicksburg. JIM LUNING

must be unconditional. Pemberton, who had served with Grant during the Mexican-American War, finally accepted his terms.

At 10 A.M. on the morning of July 4, the garrison at Vicksburg marched out from behind their lines and stacked their weapons in front of the Union Army. In total, 31,600 men surrendered, including 2,153 officers, 15 of whom were generals. Up to that time, it was the largest capture of men and artillery in the history of warfare.

The Siege of Vicksburg sometimes gets short play in comparison with other important battles of the Civil War. Perhaps this is because on July 3, as Grant was arranging an amenable surrender for Pemberton's men, another battle was heating up hundreds of miles away in Pennsylvania, outside a little town called Gettysburg.

Confederate General John Pemberton had served with General Grant during the Mexican-American War. He tried repeatedly to negotiate an honorable surrender for his men, but Grant gave him no quarter. Pemberton finally ceded on the Fourth of July, 1863. LIBRARY OF CONGRESS

The Port Gibson Bank, circa 1937. When General Ulysses S. Grant came through the town on his way to Vicksburg, he declared Port Gibson "too beautiful to burn." LIBRARY OF CONGRESS/HABS

During the Siege of Vicksburg, the city came under thunderous attack from Union artillery and gunboats. Many residents fled to nearby caves or simply dug trenches into the hillsides to protect themselves. LIBRARY OF CONGRESS

No Thanks, I'm Stuffed

When Elvis Presley was recording one of his more soupy tracks, "(Let Me Be Your) Teddy Bear," odds are he never realized the title subject was inspired by a real event, a few hundred miles south of Graceland, on Highway 61.

When President Theodore Roosevelt stopped in Onward, Mississippi, in 1902, his hosts didn't forget his reputation as an avid hunter. The area, bordered on one side by the Deer River, and on the other by miles of thick timber that would ultimately become the Delta National Forest, has long been prime hunting land. About the biggest game you can take in the area is bear.

After three days in the mosquito-infested forest, Roosevelt and company had yet to flush a bear. In frustration, his guides, with the help of dogs, ran down an elderly bear and brought it back in chains for the president to shoot. But Roosevelt, a staunch conservationist, took a look at the aged bear, already wounded by the hounds, and flatly refused.

As the story seeped out of Mississippi and into national newspapers, Clifford Berryman, a Washington, D.C., editorial cartoonist, made sport of the account in

a famed drawing captioned, "Drawing the Line in Mississippi."

In New York City, Morris Michtom, a Brooklyn shopkeeper, began selling stuffed bears his wife had made as "Teddy's bears." Today, though stuffed toys run the gamut from dinosaurs to cartoon heroes, they are still generically referred to as teddy bears.

The basic idea hasn't evolved much over the last century. This suitably ratty and primitive specimen is no doubt much like the sort that once inhabited Morris Michtom's storefront window. JOHN KOHARSKI

When President Theodore Roosevelt, on a hunting expedition near Onward, Mississippi, refused to shoot an old bear that his hunting party chained up for him to dispatch, political cartoonist Clifford Berryman immortalized the moment. LIBRARY OF CONGRESS

Though the name "teddy bear" has come to mean just about any sort of stuffed animal, the Onward Store sells reproductions of the original design. In addition, the general store is exactly that, selling hot lunches, canned goods, smokes, and gas. JIM LUNING

Thirty-odd miles north of Vicksburg is a wide spot in the road called Onward. Located just west of the Delta National Forest, it is a favorite region for hunters. JIM LUNING

A small roadside historical marker explains the details of Teddy Roosevelt's famous hunting trip for anyone who missed them back at the Onward Store. JIM LUNING

Robert Johnson: The Ghost of Mississippi

The first time I met the blues, I was sitting in the basement of a house in Mendota, Illinois. It was in a little room that my older brother Greg had carved out as his particular domain back near the furnace. It was full of Rolling Stones pictures, DayGlo paint, and most importantly, his record collection.

While he was away, I sneaked down there to revel in the sheer hippie coolness of it all and listen to his albums on what was then referred to as a "record player." I can't recall the specific date or exactly why, but eventually, I found Cream's *Wheels of Fire*. If you recall the album, it was a double LP, one record done in the studio, the other recorded live. When I finally got around to putting on the live set, the eight-year-old peach fuzz on the back of my white-boy neck literally stood on end.

The first song was "Crossroads," written by someone called Robert Johnson, a name so utterly generic to me at the time it might as well have been "John Doe" for all it revealed about its owner. But to listen to Eric Clapton's frenzied guitar was to hear a man possessed. At that age, I had no knowledge of the man who actually wrote the song or the legend surrounding it. All I knew for certain was that something was going on there that transcended a mere rock n' roll record. It was timeless, it was dangerous, and I was hooked.

In the years since, I went on to become a blues musician in my own right and the host of a well-regarded blues radio show. So as I turned off Highway 61 onto Highway 7 south of Morgan City, Mississippi, on a Sunday morning more than 30 years later, I was in many ways coming 'round the bend of an unbroken circle. I was dizzy with anticipation; my head was literally swimming.

I had a general idea of where I was going, but figured it a good bet to stop and ask directions. I eased into the parking lot of the only discernable business in Morgan City, a grocery store with windows covered in bars. Once inside, I asked the woman behind the counter if she could point me toward Mt. Zion Church.

"Services been over for two hours, you know," she said with a welcoming smile.

The LP that launched 1,000 rock bands. Columbia Records' famous 1961 reissue of Robert Johnson's recordings brought the previously forgotten bluesman to a new generation of rockers and shaped the future sound of rock n' roll to an extent that will never be quantified. JOHN KOHARSKI

The most widely known photo of Robert Johnson was a professional studio portrait showing him in a sharp suit. Years later, noted blues historian Steve LaVere discovered this photo-booth shot, which came to be known as the "dime store" photograph. Today, it is arguably more famous than the former.

"I know," I said sheepishly. "I was looking for . . ."

"I know what you looking for," she grinned. "You just git on down there where it say, 'Wildlife Preserve' and turn right. Go on now, you'll find it." And indeed I did.

Off a blacktop road there is a little country church with a graveyard to the side. And when you look carefully you see one odd-looking stone, a cenotaph actually, with a picture of a man playing the guitar and an inscribed epitaph:

Robert Johnson—King of the Delta Blues Singers

And there I paused to pay respects to the man who has become, for all intents and purposes, the eternal incarnation of the blues. There were those who had come before and legions that came after, but Johnson somehow transcended them all.

In the early 1990s, the stone at Mt. Zion was paid for by Columbia Records, which had reissued Johnson's original recordings back in 1961. Yet for all their good—albeit late—intentions, they made one rather crucial mistake: Robert Johnson isn't actually buried there.

While ironic, this seems almost fitting. In both life and death, Johnson has remained something of a ghost.

This grave in the small cemetery next to the Payne Memorial Chapel lay unmarked for decades before a rock band had a stone made, drove down, and placed it there themselves. For years, it was thought THIS was the true resting place of Robert Johnson, but new research indicates he might actually be buried on the Money Road outside Greenwood.

✦ ✦ ✦

For the record, Robert Johnson was born on May 8, 1911, in Hazlehurst, Mississippi. His mother, Julia Dodds, was actually married to someone else when she conceived a child with Noah Johnson, but such tangled relationships, however frowned upon, were as common in the rural South then as they are today.

When Johnson was still a child, he remained with the portion of his splintered family who moved north to the Mississippi Delta. By the time he reached his late teens, he had learned to play both guitar and harmonica, and since he showed little interest in school and even less in working in the fields, he applied himself to music with a vengeance. He couldn't have been in a better place; the Delta was full of musicians who traveled the area, playing at ramshackle juke joints and house parties. One of them, a Robinsonville man named Willie Brown, took Johnson under his wing, teaching him songs and ultimately introducing him to Charlie Patton—at the time, the reigning king of the Delta Blues.

By 1930 Johnson was dedicated to his music but also began to wonder about his real father, so he left the Delta and headed back south to Hazlehurst, just over 200 miles away. There, he played in jukes frequented by the road crews building highways for the Works Progress Administration. It was there he met bluesman Ike Zinnerman, who like Willie Brown, took Johnson under his wing.

In the graveyard next to the Mount Zion Church, just outside Morgan City, an obelisk pays tribute to the great blues singer Robert Johnson. Each side is carved with details about his life and recordings. Small problem—he isn't actually buried here.

Zinnerman was originally from Alabama and had always claimed he learned to play guitar while sitting on tombstones at midnight in the local cemetery. Whether he did this for inspiration or just to have a private, quiet place to learn was never really specified, but it is the kind of macabre story that sticks with a man for better or worse.

A year or so later, Johnson headed back north to the Delta, where musicians and listeners alike noticed how much his playing had improved in his absence. While it was more likely a function of practicing, playing dances, and practicing, an odd rumor began to circulate about Johnson. It is reported that fellow musician Son House first uttered the words, "He sold his soul to play like that."

The story of someone selling their soul to the Devil is an old one, dating back to African shamans and Faust alike. In the Delta, there was always a clear distinction between those musicians who played in church and those who plied their trade in juke joints. In most folks' opinion, if you weren't playing for the Lord, you were in league with the Devil.

Johnson did nothing to discourage the rumors and, in some ways, played right along with them, writing songs such as "Me and the Devil Blues," "Hellhound on my Trail," and, of course, his most famous composition, "Crossroads." Although his acclaim grew as a local performer, Johnson also wanted to make records like his idol and mentor, Charlie Patton.

A circuitous trail lead him first to Jackson, Mississippi, and the general store of H. C. Speir, who had been acting as something of a local talent scout for various record companies. Speir, dissatisfied with what the companies had been paying him, merely listened to Johnson and took down his name and address for future reference. He ultimately passed the information along to another scout named Ernie Oertle, who tracked down Johnson and took him to San Antonio, Texas, for recording sessions in November 1936 and June 1937.

Johnson recorded 29 compositions during those sessions; 22 of them were released during his lifetime. Although their sales never made him rich, they did open up new audiences to him, and soon Johnson was traveling and playing not only in the Delta, but also as far away as New York City and Windsor, Ontario. But it was in Mississippi that Johnson had his first and most loyal fan base, and it was there where he paused in August 1938 to visit his family and friends before venturing farther south.

Johnson was booked to play in a juke joint outside of Greenwood, a little place known locally as Three Forks, with Sonny Boy Williamson and David "Honeyboy" Edwards. Johnson had been in the area for a few weeks and began showing some interest in the juke owner's wife. Although Johnson might have been oblivious to the danger, Williamson sensed a bad situation developing as they began playing.

When the two took a break, someone brought Johnson a half-pint of whiskey with a broken seal. Williamson quickly slapped it out of his hand before he could take a drink and warned him about the danger of drinking from an opened bottle. Johnson merely scolded the harmonica player for wasting the liquor and was soon brought another bottle. Its seal was also broken, and Johnson drank freely.

When he and Williamson went back to playing, Johnson didn't last more than a few songs. He stopped in the middle of a number and staggered outside, violently ill. He was taken back to Greenwood, where he lay at death's door before finally succumbing to pneumonia, brought on by weakness from arsenic poisoning, on August 16, 1938. On his death certificate, the cause of death is listed as simply "No Doctor," while on the reverse, a bit of scandalous hearsay suggests he died of syphilis.

A side trip up Highway 7 from Morgan City to Quito, site of Payne Memorial Chapel. JIM LUNING

And so it might have ended, Johnson taken at an early age, his records falling out of print one by one with nothing left but a shadowy legend of a great man. But a tiny group of record collectors preserved those early 78s, and soon blues aficionados heard whispers of the mystery man from Mississippi who perhaps had sold his soul to Satan in return for such unearthly talent. In 1961, Columbia released a collection of Johnson's seminal tracks, and while the LP's audience at that time comprised mostly folkies and musicologists, it was a groundbreaking release. Like many other obscure records, it seems everyone who heard it went on to form a band.

As rock bands began re-recording Johnson's songs, there grew a wider audience for the original recordings. Columbia released a second album of his original tracks, and the story behind the music came to the forefront.

In 1986, that story was made into a perfectly awful movie called *Crossroads*, starring Ralph Macchio as Eugene Martone, a classical guitar prodigy who really wants to be a bluesman. It even called the character of the aging musician who takes Eugene under his wing Willie Brown. Although in a broad sense it might have sparked some interest in Johnson's music, it ended up being more a story of teenage lust and rebellion than a true paean to the blues.

In 1990, with the advent of digital remastering, Columbia released the complete recordings of Robert Johnson on compact disc. This box set, with authoritative liner notes by Steve LaVere and gushing praise from the likes of Keith Richards and Eric Clapton, among others, is the best introduction to the man and his music to date. Short of an actual resurrection, it is likely the last we will hear.

◆　◆　◆

And it was Volume One of this collection that boomed out the windows of the van as I made my way out of Morgan City, looking for what I had heard was the actual resting place of Robert Johnson, a little churchyard in Quito, a few miles north.

There is no sign telling you the few houses that remain are actually a town, but a quick look down a bumpy dirt and gravel road reveals the sign for the Payne Memorial Chapel. There, in the side yard are a number of graves, a few fresh but most old and apparently forgotten. Only one stone is covered in guitar picks.

The sun was blisteringly hot, and when I touched my hand to the stone, it felt as if was heated from below. I removed the guitar picks from the stone's surface and quickly made a few rubbings of the epitaph; the hot stone quickly melting the crayons I was using. I carefully replaced the picks and notes left by other pilgrims and, still dizzy, swept back onto the main road toward Itta Bena.

It was a few months later that I learned researchers recently discovered evidence indicating that Johnson was not actually buried in Quito, either, but farther north, along what is known as the "Money Road," outside of Greenwood. (Until this revelation, the town of Money, Mississippi, was known mostly as the place where, in 1955, 14-year-old Emmett Till allegedly whistled at a white woman. A few days later, he was visited by a group of white men. A few days after that, his mutilated body was found in a swamp, a cotton gin fan tied around his neck with barbed wire. *Jet* magazine ran pictures of him in an open coffin, and the horrible murder became a lightning rod for the civil rights movement, fueling outrage among black and white Americans, alike.)

You can now visit three different gravesites when searching for Robert Johnson, and whether he is actually under any one of them is anybody's guess.

Perhaps it is best left that way. Although a wealth of information has surfaced about Johnson over the years, he still seems larger than life itself. In a way, hearing the details of his day-to-day life in and around Mississippi seems to chip away at the icon he has rightly become.

Regardless, I know deep down inside that one of these days I am going to return to Mississippi and look for that little church on the Money Road.

Robert Johnson's death certificate lists the cause of death is listed as simply "No Doctor." On the reverse, a bit of scandalous hearsay suggests he died of syphilis. ©1986

Hudson Essex Terraplane

There are several universal themes in the blues, and the ones that don't have to do with broom-dusting, getting up in the morning, or drinking are usually about cars. "Pontiac Blues," "Mercury Blues," "V-8 Ford," and "Broke Down Engine," all conjure the automobile as their muse. But the granddaddy of them all is Robert Johnson's "Terraplane Blues."

Though any true blues fan knows the song, fewer know exactly what a damned Terraplane is. The Hudson Terraplane was introduced on July 21, 1932, in a grand ceremony broadcast live from Detroit. As part of the great unveiling, a female pilot smashed a bottle of aviation fuel across the hood, declaring, "I christen thee Essex Terraplane." Her name was Amelia Earhart.

The song was Johnson's first bona fide hit and it made him a regional star—as well as the envy of many of the older bluesmen he had learned from. Of course, when in the song, Johnson complained that someone had been driving his Terraplane, he wasn't talking about a car . . . at least not any more than Muddy Waters was talking about a half-breed horse when he complained about another mule kicking in his stall. They were simple double entendres about cheating women.

In an odd twist, Hudson discontinued the Terraplane model in 1938, the same year Johnson died.

A Terraplane badge adorns this 1937's toothy grille. While stylish by some more recent bar-of-soap styling standards, Terraplanes were actually at the bottom of the Hudson food chain. JON ROBINSON

One of Johnson's first and best-known recordings is the wonderful "Terraplane Blues." COURTESY ROBERT JOHNSON COLLECTION, GREENWOOD BLUES HERITAGE MUSEUM & GALLERY, GREENWOOD, MISSISSIPPI

Vocalion

Not Licensed for Radio Broadcast (SA 2586)

Vocal Blues with Guitar Acc.

TERRAPLANE BLUES
—Robert Johnson—
ROBERT JOHNSON

03416

U.S.PAT. 1,677,544 BRUNSWICK RECORD CORPORATION

It's doubtful Johnson was referring to the plugs atop the Terraplane's 112ci six-cylinder flathead when he sang, "And when I mash down your little starter/ Then your spark plug will give me a fire." TERRAPLANE PHOTOS COURTESY OF JON ROBINSON

All Hudsons built in 1937 featured a redesigned instrument panel with what was essentially an upside-down speedometer; the needle started at zero near the top right and rotated in clockwise until it reached top speed, in this case as high as 90 miles per hour, at the top left. The feature proved unpopular and was discontinued for 1938.

This 1937 Super Terraplane Sedan, built a couple years after Johnson recorded "Terraplane Blues," was a couple steps up from the Deluxe model in that it featured such amenities as a radio and patterned upholstery.

"I even flash my lights mama/This horn won't even blow/Got a short in this connection/ Ooh well, babe, it's way down below," sang Johnson—which could prove a problem when dealing with tailgaters, considering most Terraplanes, this Deluxe being an exception, had just one taillight.

This Terraplane probably cost its original owner in the neighborhood of $725 when bought new. Its generous 117-inch wheelbase endowed the car with a smooth ride, justifying its name, literraly translaated as "grounded flight."

A Hudson Terraplane of the sort memorialized by Johnson.
COURTESY ROBERT JOHNSON COLLECTION, GREENWOOD BLUES HERITAGE MUSEUM & GALLERY, GREENWOOD, MISSISSIPPI

Riverside Hotel: "You're at Home Now"

Frank "Rat" Ratliff, proprietor of the Riverside. He took over operation of the place after his mother passed away. "You're at home now," he assures guests in a soothing Delta drawl. The Riverside Hotel cannot be recommended highly enough if you are a blues disciple. JIM LUNING.

A few blocks south of the crossroads of Highways 61 and 49, I turned west onto Sunflower Avenue looking for a place I had read about. I had seen a couple pictures of it before, but they were both strictly street level, and I couldn't rightly tell from the images if the building had more than one story or even what side of the street it was on, for that matter. So, I wasn't actually expecting to find the Riverside Hotel, and then it turned out that I found it. A simple red, white, and blue bunting decorated the sign over the front door.

✦　　✦　　✦

It was a lazy Delta afternoon, with the sun beating down on everything and the Sunflower River flowing slow and muddy behind the place.

A metal-barred door opened down a dark hallway and out stepped proprietor Frank Ratliff, his eyes still adjusting to the sharp sunlight streaming into the hallway. My eyes had yet to adjust, so I couldn't see him, but I could hear the smile in his voice.

"Hey, man! How you doing, Tim?" he asked. "I knew from when we talked on the phone you would come."

It seemed an odd thing to say, and I wouldn't realize exactly what he was talking about until later.

Ratliff escorted me across the hall into what, this far south, could rightly be called a parlor. The coffee table was strewn with books and newspaper articles. There was an old Peavey 410 amplifier and an older-still Airline guitar leaning against it. Behind both was an aged metal suitcase.

Ratliff slipped into a chair, draping one leg over its arm, and lit a menthol 100.

"Rat," as he insists being called, is the son of the Riverside's legendary proprietor, "Mother" Z. L. Hill, who began running the place just after it was converted into a hotel in the 1940s.

The building was originally the G. T. Thomas Afro-American Hospital, the only place in the area where blacks could receive serious medical care. What is now room two was once the hospital's operating room. Rat won't rent it out unless he is completely full. It is something of a shrine.

On the night of September 26, 1937, singer Bessie Smith was driving from Memphis to Clarksdale after a show. Although the details tend to take on a life of their own after so many years, this much is known. Smith's car smashed into the back of a truck, and she was thrown from the vehicle. It's thought that while she lay in the road gravely injured, she was run over by another truck that didn't even slow down.

After her death, a rumor began to circulate that she had been taken to several white hospitals that night and was refused treatment. While some say record producer John Hammond started the rumor, it grew to become essentially an urban legend after musicologist Alan Lomax repeated it in his book, *The Land Where the Blues Began*.

But the truth seems to be that she was brought directly to what is now the Riverside and treated by a white doctor. With one arm almost completely sev-

Located at 615 Sunflower in Clarksdale, the Riverside Hotel swims in blues history and Delta hospitality. Some of the most legendary performers of the era stayed here off and on. In fact, one of the most legendary among them died here. JIM LUNING

ered, she had already lost so much blood that there was little the doctor could do but make her comfortable. The Empress of the Blues, just 43 years old, died a few hours later. She was buried near her home in Pennsylvania after a lavish funeral.

There is a picture of Smith on the wall of room two and a poster lying on the bed that Rat has been meaning to hang up. It's a modest shrine, but a heartfelt one all the same. For that reason alone, the Riverside would be sanctified ground to a blues fan, but after the place was converted into a black-only hotel, some of the blues' greatest legends began passing through its doors while en route between St. Louis and New Orleans. It was the place where the likes of Howlin' Wolf, Ike Turner, Pinetop Perkins, and Robert Nighthawk would call it a night after playing a club in Memphis or a local party. It was also popular with travelers passing up and down Highway 61, located a few blocks away.

In a spot of irony, the building went from being the last place a black man in Clarksdale usually stayed, to the first place he would go once he got there. Heidegger would have a field day with that one.

The Empress of the Blues, Bessie Smith, was the original belter, a woman who could shake dust out the timbers of a nightclub. She died at the Riverside Hotel on September 26, 1937. LIBRARY OF CONGRESS

✦   ✦   ✦

Rat watched them come and go over the years, the famous and nameless alike, always working in the background while Mother Hill dealt with the guests. Since everyone called her "Mother," she called the guests her "boys." Answering, "My boy will take care of it," simply meant one of the guests was going to deal with changing a light bulb, picking up her lunch downtown, or whatever needed doing at the moment.

An old registration card from the Riverside's heyday. The guest register is legendary, holding the signatures of several blues legends, modern musicians, and celebrities. You can only sign the register if you stay at the hotel. COURTESY FRANK "RAT" RATLIFF AND THE RIVERSIDE HOTEL

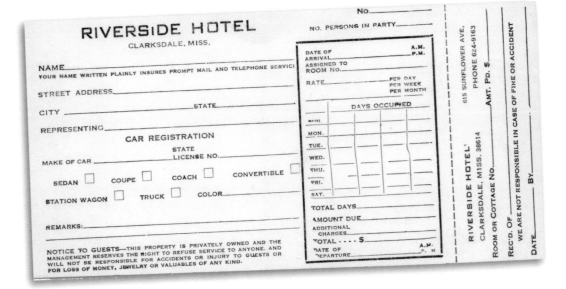

Room number two at the Riverside. Many years before, when the building was used as a hospital, this was an operating room. It is where the great singer Bessie Smith died after being involved in an auto accident north of Clarksdale. JIM LUNING

So one morning back in 1991, when Rat called down to the hotel to see if Mother Hill wanted him to bring her something to eat, and she answered, "My boy is getting it," he didn't think twice.

"You'll love this," Rat chuckled as he scrunched over in his chair as if what he was about to reveal was to be kept in close confidence.

"So I got down to the hotel and went into Mama's room, and there she is sitting there with nothing to eat.

"'I thought your boy was gonna get your lunch?' I asked.

"'He's just gone,' she says.

"And right about then, this big white boy comes walking in and hands Mama some lunch and then plops up on her bed and starts eating." Rat paused in the story and leaned over even farther.

"Now I just thought this was hiiiiigh-ly unusual," he said, stretching the word into an almost comic delivery

"I mean, she don't even let *me* get up on her bed like that! Who the hell is this white boy sittin' all up in my mama's bed?"

Mother Hill did chide her guest about putting his feet on her bed once, but other than that, they got along famously. Her boy was there for a few days checking out the Sunflower River Blues Festival but always managed to visit with her between his comings and goings.

It was the last night of the festival when Rat happened to call Mother Hill about one thing or another. As they were hanging up, Mother Hill popped a quick question.

"You *do* know who my boy is don't you?" she asked Rat.

"I don't know. Looks like just some white boy to me," he said, not sure what she meant.

"You fool, that's John Jr.," she said.

"John who?"

"John F. Kennedy Jr.," Mother Hill told him.

Kennedy had come down for the festival and was booked into the place by his friend, Howard Stovall (executive director of The Blues Foundation and descendant of the famous Mississippi cotton growers, incidentally, one-time employers of Muddy Waters), who knew he would be both well cared for and left alone. The local newspaper was a bit embarrassed about missing Clarksdale's famous visitor, who reportedly spent much of the weekend walking around town unrecognized.

Later, when asked why she didn't immediately spread the word when she realized who her guest was, Mother Hill simply replied, "Ain't nobody's business."

◆ ◆ ◆

After his mother died in 1997, Rat took over the place and now caters to a mix of workingmen, retirees, and blues tourists who keep the place full but rarely filled. He doesn't accept credit cards and isn't all that crazy about taking reservations, for that matter. The main line to the hotel rings out in the hallway.

The crossroads at which Johnson supposedly sold his soul were out in the country, but in Clarksdale, Mississippi, the intersection of Highways 61 and 49 have become known as THE *crossroads for legions of misguided blues tourists.*
JIM LUNING

Clarksdale: Walking in Jerusalem

It's the town where it all started and nothing ever changed. It's the unofficial county seat of the Mississippi Delta, and the true Jerusalem of the Church of the Delta Blues. Coming here is something of a *hadj*, a religious journey, and if strolling down Issaqueena Street feels vaguely familiar once you finally come here, it is because, like most people who seek out this particular corner of Mississippi, you have been here in spirit for years.

Were it not for Robert Johnson, it would probably be simply an intersection, but the spot where Highway 61 and 49 meet in Clarksdale has always been known as "the crossroads"—*the* Crossroads, that mythical place where Johnson sold his soul. Nothing could be further from the truth.

There is a monument of sorts for the legend, with a guitar and crossed signs beneath. On the northeast corner, Abe's Barbecue has been serving up hot pulled pork and smoked brisket for decades. Next door is a liquor store where, having slid your money into a wooden drawer from which the clerk, shielded behind a layer of bulletproof glass, can retrieve and count it, you can cop a drink.

Of course, were you to stop by a neighborhood joint in Clarksdale and tell them you were visiting "the crossroads," you would likely get a kind smile and nod much akin to if you had just said you were on the trail of Bigfoot. But like the plantations in St. Francisville, the blues in Clarksdale have become a commodity—perhaps the only commodity besides cotton.

Rat pointed the way outside to the shaded porch in front of the place. There were some old-fashioned metal lawn chairs aligned in a row—none of that coordinated white molded resin business but good old painted steel leaning this way and that, still as strong as the day they were made.

As we leaned back into the cool shade, a car pulled up in front of the hotel and a youngish-looking man hopped out and made his way toward us. Rat leaned up in his chair with a smile.

"Say, man, this is Nate. He's like my second-in-command around here," Rat explained. "If you don't see me, you see him. Got that?"

Nate shifted the paper sack in his arm and gave a wave as he headed in the front door. He returned a few minutes later with a tall boy of Colt .45 and plopped into a chair out front. He sat, silently paging through the copy of a Route 66 book I had given Rat, and then looked up.

"Let me ask you something," he said with a wry smile.

"Shoot," I said.

"You all see any black people out there on Route 66?" he asked, flipping through the pages, back to front this time.

"Yeah, some I guess," I answered. "Why?"

"Well you're about to see a whole mess of them around here," he laughed, taking a sip from his beer.

A car slowly pulled by, stopping for a moment in front of the place. The windows were tinted slightly, but I could make out people pointing. Rat waved to the unseen driver. The car pulled away slowly, heading west into downtown Clarksdale.

"They'll stay out on the highway, I bet," said Nate.

"Out on the highway" means out on Highway 61, where a crop of chain motels and fast food places draw the bulk of the tourist business away from the Riverside and downtown Clarksdale.

Though the occasional kindred spirit will stop and actually spend the night in the place, more often than not, they just stop, take a picture, and keep moving.

One of the Riverside's more noted guests, John F. Kennedy Jr. His friend, Howard Stovall (left), assured him he would be well taken care of there. Kennedy reportedly roamed around Clarksdale all weekend, enjoying the 1991 Sunflower River Blues Festival unrecognized. COURTESY HOWARD STOVALL

"You know what cracks me up?" Rat asked, looking over at Nate and me. "It's the ones that won't even get out of the car. They roll down the window this little tiny crack and stick a camera out, and then off they go. I don't know what the hell's wrong with those people."

For the investor types out there, the Riverside is for sale. And Rat has a simple equation to work out a fair price.

"You take a school bus and park it out here," he said with a sly grin.

"You take out all the seats, and I mean every seat, driver's included. Then you fill it to the roof with hundred-dollar bills, 'til you can't fit nothing else in there. Then you can talk to me about selling this place.

"They started calling when my mama died. All these people sayin' they wanted to buy it for this reason or that," Rat said with an air of disgust. "I told them all, 'This is a family business.'" After which he summarily hung up on them.

JAMES FEISER, ACTING NATIONAL CHAIRMAN, AMERICAN RED CROSS; HERBERT HOOVER, SECRETARY OF COMMERCE, AND DWIGHT DAVIS, SECRETARY OF WAR
Photographed at Vicksburg while on tour of inspection of refugee camps

Floods have ravaged the Delta region for hundreds of years. One of the worst in memory was the Great Flood of 1927 that sent a slow, brown wave of destruction along the length of the Mississippi. Here, President Herbert Hoover visits a flooded Vicksburg. LIBRARY OF CONGRESS

Shack Up Inn: Hopson Plantation

The directions, although they turned out to be wrong, seemed simple enough: Head west on Highway 49 for about a mile and a half until you see the old cotton gin. After a few miles, it became pretty obvious that I had gone farther than necessary, but something else dawned on me as I reached the outskirts of Clarksdale: I had no idea what a cotton gin looked like.

My only experience with the things had been a chapter on Eli Whitney back in high school history class. I knew it was some sort of separating machine and figured, in the age of mass production, it had probably grown larger than whatever Whitney had bolted together in his workshop. I figured whatever it was I was looking for would be larger than a Datsun, with bales of cotton issuing out one end like a hay baler up north.

I tried calling the folks out at the plantation again to check the directions, but got no answer, so I tried heading west on 49 instead of east and eventually found the remnants of Hopson Plantation exactly where it should have been in the first place.

What I quickly realized as I pulled down the recently graded gravel road was that a "gin" in this part of the country is not a machine but a factory unto itself. And this plantation is where the cotton industry, and the face of the South, had changed forever.

✦ ✦ ✦

Inside the old commissary building is a respectable juke joint that, although it keeps erratic hours during the week, is the real deal. The old wagon sheds have been converted into an office, lounge, lending library, and main residence for one of the owners. Beyond that is a line of restored sharecropper shacks that they operate as the Shack Up Inn.

I suppose there is a moment where you need to wonder whether re-creating the cotton plantation experience for blues tourists might not piss off someone somewhere. I suppose if they had actors out there picking cotton,

The interior of one of the Shack Up Inn's cabins features an old (as in, OLD) Coca-Cola machine converted to a refrigerator, a vintage sideboard, and a hand-hewn bed frame in the next room. A note left on the stove by a repairman advises guests not to use the oven if they value their lives. JIM LUNING

These Hopson Plantation shacks were saved and renovated as the Shack Up Inn's guest cottages. The owners were sure to make them comfortable, but not too comfortable. For example, they left the cracks in the floor but installed a layer of fine screen beneath to keep out mosquitoes. JIM LUNING

it would come off as politically incorrect, but if there is offense taken here, it is strictly of the "Hogan's Heroes" variety.

The shacks are deceptively comfortable and furnished with a funky mix of fixtures, from a rough-hewn four-poster bed, to an old—as in, *really* old—Coca-Cola machine for a refrigerator. There is a Moon Pie on your pillow.

Back in the 1940s, Hopson was cranking out cotton for the war effort and was always in danger of losing its workers to the military. Blues piano legend Pinetop Perkins spent his time during the war driving a tractor on Hopson. Today, there is a shack that bears his name. One day a few years back, Perkins came to see the place and ended up staying the night.

"I remember he got up the next morning real early and just sat on the porch for the longest time. Didn't say a word. Just sat there with this big smile on his face," said Bill Talbot, one of the owning partners.

It is a loosely run affair, with one or more of the partners around, usually. Bill runs a pool business in the mornings; James Butler rolls in after he gets off work at five. They keep the bar open until everyone

leaves, usually. When I told James I had to head into town and wouldn't be back until later, he informed me he would be gone but would leave the door open if I wanted a drink later. It's that kind of place.

One of the bedrooms in the shack features an old claw-foot table, oak office chairs, plus a satellite TV and radio receiver. You get one channel: the Blues Station. Jim Luning

A respectable juke joint featuring live music most weekends has sprung up inside the old commissary building on Hopson Plantation, now the Shack Up Inn in Clarksdale. Chock full of antiques, the jukes' hours are essentially from whenever someone decides to show up to when the bartender is ready to go home. Jim Luning

Super Chikan

Close your eyes for second and conjure up a picture of an authentic Mississippi bluesman. What do you see? A suit with creases sharp enough to cut you at 50 paces? A pair of hands gnarled from years of hard work and fistfights? Perhaps a face weathered by cheap whiskey and years of work under the Delta sun? Is he sitting on the porch of a rundown shack, surrounded by cotton fields? Now open your eyes.

The Super Chikan had just got home from work as a truck driver and was still wearing the shirt with his name emblazoned over one pocket. He was hustling a lawn mower back and forth in front of his standard ranch-style house on the south side of Clarksdale, trying to beat both an approaching rainstorm and the return of his wife and family.

He killed the engine on the mower and greeted me, looking at his watch.

"I was wondering where you was," he said with a hearty laugh. "Then I heard your muffler down the block and said 'Whoop . . . there he go.'"

The Super Chikan is a modern practitioner of the blues, and one with a critical ear when it comes to modern players. Once, he sat in the office of a blues record label head after listening to a demo tape. The label head was enthusiastic and said he thought the demo was quite good. The Super Chikan just looked at him quizzically.

"You call that singin'?" he asked, incredulous. "I think you had something bad for breakfast, man."

The demo tape consisted of some homemade recordings done on a cheap four-track recorder. The artist in question was a fellow from Clarksdale named James Johnson. His friends and fans know him as . . . Super Chikan.

James Louis Johnson was born in 1951, the nephew of another Clarksdale legend, Big Jack "The Oilman"

Super Chikan with one of his famous "Chik-can-tars" that he builds from old military-issue gas cans. In addition, he performs live and does wonderful folk-art paintings of Delta life, some of which have been displayed at the Delta Blues Museum in Clarksdale. JIM LUNING

For years, Delta's Stackhouse, a record store on Sunflower in Clarksdale, was run by renowned blues preservationist Jim O'Neal, who also operated a record label and magazine out of the unique building. JIM LUNING

Johnson. Even given that pedigree, James gave little thought to ever following in his uncle's footsteps.

"I had just been playing around with it really," he said. "I never had any intention of becoming a musician. I was just always messing with the stuff. But I heard a guy talking on the radio one day, and he was saying how songwriters made more money than the performers. So I started writing songs, thinking maybe someone would want to sing them.

The former Greyhound station in downtown Clarksdale has long been a point of departure for countless people headed north in search of better jobs, better living conditions, better weather, or usually all of the above. JIM LUNING

"You call that singin'? I think you had something bad for breakfast, man."

— *James "Super Chikan" Johnson*

"I had my own little homemade overdubbing setup at home. I use that little DD5 [electronic drum machine] over there for a time machine. So I would dub it all onto regular old cassette tape. One day I went down there and talked to Jim O'Neal at Rooster Records here in Clarksdale, down at the Stackhouse. I said I had been writing some songs and here's what they sound like, and I got the words wrote out on paper and tape of the music. I figured someone might hear it and get an idea and want to record it. Just give me credit for the song.

Abe's Bar B Q has been dishing up smoked brisket and pulled pork at the crossroads of Highway 61 and 49 in Clarksdale since 1924. JIM LUNING

Aleck Miller, who went by the name Sonny Boy Williamson, is buried in this secluded cemetery a few miles outside Tutwiler, Mississippi. Almost impossible to find with out a detailed map, it is visited regularly by pilgrims who leave harmonicas and bottles of liquor. Legend has it that if you show up at midnight on a certain day of the year, Williamson's ghost will jump up and play you a tune.

Super Chikan's Chik-can-tar
By Scott Coopwood

Super Chikan has made a name for himself around the North Delta playing the blues with his band. Anyone that has ever seen Chikan play his guitar will tell you that he is one bad guitar player—and that means good. However, some of Chikan's fans would be surprised to learn that not only is he a dedicated guitar player, he is also a dedicated inventor and folk artist. In the late 1990s, Chikan invented a guitar that is made from a five-gallon military gas can. To add to his "Chik-can-tars," Chikan began painting them in interesting ways using his folk-art touch. The results are amazing in sound and in look.

"When I was a kid, I experimented with making 'bucket guitars' and other things back then," says Chikan. "I finally started making them out of metal gas cans when I got older, thinking that, with the hole of the gas can on the end, all a player would have to do is stick a microphone over the hole and sing at the same time. The microphone would pick up both."

Music and art have been in Chikan's family for some time. Growing up around the Clarksdale area, Chikan was introduced to music at an early age.

"My grandaddy was a fiddler, my uncle Big Jack played guitar, and they would all sit around and play music with their friends," says Chikan. "When I was a little boy, I'd sit around and listen to them play. I was never allowed to mess with their guitars, but I was fascinated by all of it. I made my first guitar with a board and a piece of bailing wire—a diddley bow is what they called it then."

Chikan says that he learned to play the guitar easily and that he listened to many kinds of music growing up: "I always liked several kinds of music and that's why my music today sounds so different."

To add a personal touch to his creations, Chikan has decorated them with scenes from his Quitman County childhood, as well as a depiction of the crossroads deal between Robert Johnson and the Devil.

The Blue and White Restaurant on Highway 61 in Tunica serves up righteous amounts of catfish, barbecue sandwiches, and general fare. It comes highly recommended by locals and Memphis folks alike. JIM LUNING

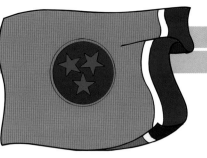

"Well he listened to them and he said, 'Why don't you sing them yourself?'

"I said, 'Well, first of all, I can't sing. Second of all, I don't have a band. And third of all, I can't afford the studio time.'"

O'Neal assured him he could take care of the band and studio problems, but Johnson still insisted he couldn't sing.

"Well I just heard you singing them on that tape," said O'Neal.

"You call that singing? I was just making noise about an idea of it."

"Well it sounds pretty good to me," O'Neal persisted.

Next thing he knew, Johnson had a record deal.

As for the nickname, he had grown up around chickens, feeding them and taking care of them in general, and was known as "Chicken Boy." Then it sort of took on a life of its own.

"I got a job driving a taxi cab and the dispatcher would call me 'Fast Red.' Finally, one day somebody told him my name was Chicken, and he said, 'Well, he's a fast chicken.'

"Then they started calling me 'Quick Chicken,' then 'Super Fast Chicken.' Then it got all mixed up and they would ask for 'Super Chicken.'"

Johnson has taken all the permutations in stride.

"I've been called worse," he laughed.

And while he has played as far off as Chicago and Duluth, Johnson has been humble about his new career.

"I don't know anything about music. I can't read or write music. Whatever sounds good to me is what I like to play. Someone might come along later and say, 'Hey, that's New Orleans–style music,' or country or whatever. I just say, 'No, that's Super Chikan music.'"

Casinos near Tunica have taken over a landscape once dominated by sharecropper shacks and endless cotton fields. Gambling licenses in Mississippi are a fraction of the cost they are elsewhere, and Tunica has become a favorite side trip for travelers heading toward Memphis. Though the gambling industry pumps cash into the town of Tunica itself, unincorporated areas to the north are still scraping by in abject poverty.
JIM LUNING

🛡61 Act II: Memphis to Dubuque

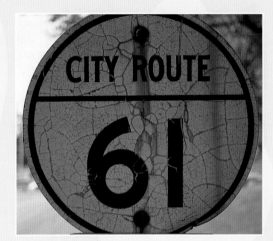

A very old city route sign marks Highway 61 on the southern edge of Dubuque, Iowa.

Nighttime on old Beale Street. Once the buzzing center of Memphis, it has been re-born into a vibrant, if somewhat tamer, ver-sion of the original entertainment district. JIM LUNING

This is the bridge.

To a musician, a bridge is a chunk tossed in for eight bars to break up the groove a bit, add some diversity, and turn the listener's interest to what lies at the end. In creating a bridge, a musician typically changes the key, just to make it sound and feel different.

This is Missouri and Iowa.

Were it not for the primary elections held there, Iowa might universally be consid-ered—rightly or wrongly—as the least important place in America. Missouri has some issues, too, but at least it has St. Louis.

South of St. Louis, you walk in the footsteps of French explorers who passed through the area hundreds of years ago. North of St. Louis, you walk in the footsteps of Tom Sawyer. Cross the border into Keokuk, Iowa, and you are sucking down grape Nehis with Radar O' Reilly.

You cross Highway 61's bridge, into the middle eight, with reduced expectations. There is Budweiser and there is corn. Somewhere down the line, there will be Wisconsin.

But like any good riddle, Highway 61 offers a different ending than the one you might expect. There is a guy with a guitar up ahead. There is a woman who would like to bum a smoke. You meet each with open ears, open eyes, and an open heart.

Graceland: One King to Rule Them All

Elvis Presley is pop-culture monolith, with slight variations. Somewhere along the line, the true believers connect with either the young or old Elvis, the Memphis or Vegas Elvis, the tousled-boy-from-Tupelo Elvis or the rich-fat-guy-dead-on-his-crapper Elvis. To the rest of us less invested in the man and his many myths, he remains an old publicity photo or a jerky dance number from a B movie.

But the sad, bloated caricature he ultimately became, the indignity of his death, and the corporate machine that, for almost 30 years after his death, continues to rake in millions of dollars annually, all fade to the background when you walk through the gates of the palace.

Graceland.

The spare bedroom at Graceland looks out over the eastern grounds of the estate. JIM LUNING

Home to 1,001 fried peanut-butter-and-banana sandwiches: Elvis' kitchen. JIM LUNING

◆ ◆ ◆

A local doctor built the 23-room colonial mansion on land that had been in his family for over a century. Named after the physician's wife, it was erected on what was then Bellevue Avenue in Memphis, Tennessee. In 1972, Bellevue's name was changed to Elvis Presley Boulevard.

Many years ago, I was stationed in Memphis, and when some old hometown friends decided to visit for one weekend, one of the places they insisted on seeing was Graceland.

It was just a few years after Presley died, and the place was not open to the public. You could stroll up to the entrance, though, and peer in through the wrought-iron gates and imagine what might lie beyond. But that was about it.

Across the street from the mansion was a typical-looking strip mall, the sort of place you can find all over the country, populated by dry cleaners, takeout Chinese places, and cut-rate travel agencies. But this one, all eight or nine storefronts, contained nothing but Elvis souvenirs. There were Elvis ashtrays and doorknockers, every kind of T-shirt one could imagine, even Elvis toilet paper, for those who really wanted to be close to the King.

These days, the sprawling compound across the street from Graceland is like a mini–Disney World. There is an auto museum featuring several of Presley's cars. There are two airliners parked outside. And there are lines, everyday, all the time: up to 4,000 people a day and over 600,000 a year. Pilgrims from all over the world are packed into a fleet of shuttles, driven across the street, and given the cook's tour of the old estate.

It is an oddly private moment to see, when they step off the shuttle and connect with their own personal Elvis. There are the few that invariably whip out cell phones and begin making calls ("Hey, Merle! Guess where I'm at?!"), but more often a hushed reverence overcomes them. They speak in whispers, pointing out the furnishings, debating what might have happened in one room or the other.

Welcome to the jungle. Once upon a time, it was fashionable to have a jungle room. Thankfully, I think, that time has passed. JIM LUNING

Once inside, the tour guide explains that flash photography is prohibited (prompting most of the pilgrims to look down at their digital cameras in a confused panic), and that the tour will not include the upstairs, which Elvis considered his *sancto sanctorum.*

To be fair, the décor is frozen in time, a flash of late-1960s fabulous. There are a few classic pieces, but taken as a whole, the interior is an example of what must have seemed elegant to a poor, white Southerner circa 1957.

There is a "formal" living room to the right, and the dining room, where Elvis is said to have held court with his guests, is to the left. Meandering through the house, you see the kitchen and the "jungle room," and eventually wind your way downstairs to the billiard room and the "media room," with its bank of TV screens installed in one wall.

Continuing outside, one passes through Presley's father's office, the "smokehouse," which was converted to a shooting range, then eventually to the gravesites.

Presley was originally buried in Forest Hill Cemetery in Memphis, but the stream of visitors and concerns about security led to his remains being moved to Graceland in 1979. In all, there are four Presleys resting here: Elvis; his mother, Gladys; his father, Vernon; and his little-known, stillborn twin, Jesse. Elvis' only child, Lisa Marie, who oversees the handling of various Presley enterprises in addition to her budding music career, says she will likely be buried there as well.

The graves are the last stop on the circuitous tour, and the pilgrims, some misty-eyed, pause to pay their respects before sauntering slowly back to the shuttle, which drives them back across the street, depositing them in front of the gift shops.

✦ ✦ ✦

Navigating out of the parking lot and onto Elvis Presley Boulevard, I make my way back west toward Highway 61, then head north toward Mulberry Street, where another King died.

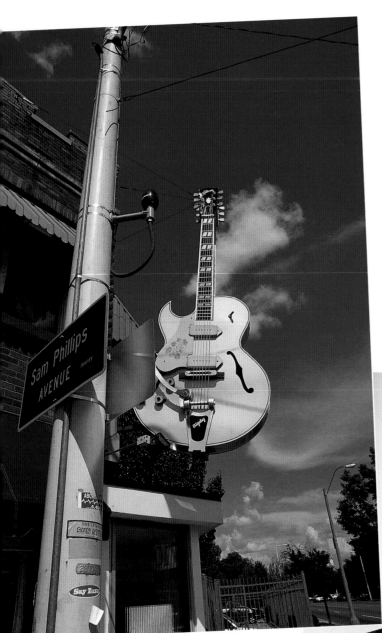

Inside this building, producer Sam Phillips, Elvis' first record producer, created a sound that fueled everything from the Beatles and Rolling Stones to Southern Culture on the Skids. JIM LUNING

Elvis Presley is buried next to his mother, father, and stillborn twin brother. He was originally buried in Memphis proper but was moved here a few years later for security reasons. JIM LUNING

Once out of the residence proper, the tour leads through a small museum, featuring Elvis' gold records, copies of various letters and checks he wrote, and a number of his outfits. JIM LUNING

In the basement of Graceland, Elvis's billiard room features an overstuffed couch for spectators and a rather bizarre fabric ceiling treatment. JIM LUNING

Lorraine Motel: The End of the Dream

No matter how old you were when it actually happened, you've seen the picture—one man down, three people pointing across a motel railing to a building across the street. It was April 4, 1968, and the man lying on the balcony, mortally wounded, was Dr. Martin Luther King Jr.

Back in March, King had come to Memphis to mediate a strike by the city's sanitation workers. He called for a citywide work stoppage and promised to return to lead a nonviolent protest. Due to a freak snowstorm that paralyzed the city on March 22, King's march on city hall was delayed to March 28.

As the crowds arrived at city hall around 11:30 that morning, a riot broke out, injuring over 60 people and leaving one person dead, shot by police. By nightfall, thousands of National Guard troops took to the street, hoping to prevent the chaos and looting that could follow.

The next day, King left Memphis, once again promising to come back and lead another demonstration. On April 3, he returned and moved into his usual room at the Lorraine Motel, number 306-7, a suite he had shared so often with his friend, Reverend Ralph Abernathy, that his associates referred to it as the "King-Abernathy Suite."

That night, King spoke before a packed house at the Mason Temple, delivering his momentous and eerily predictive "I've Been to the Mountaintop" speech.

The next evening, King was scheduled to have dinner with friends at 5:00 P.M. Running late, he stepped out

Though the sign still reads Lorraine Motel, the interior of the building is now officially the National Civil Rights Museum. One of the stops on the tour is room 307, where Dr. Martin Luther King Jr. was staying the night he was assassinated on the motel balcony.
JIM LUNING

A view of Memphis from the top of the world-famous Peabody Hotel, renowned for the ducks that live in its lobby fountain. The ducks have a special cage on the roof and are marched to and from "work" each day by a duckmaster.
JIM LUNING

Civil rights leaders on the balcony of the Lorraine Motel point in the direction of the gunman moments after the assassination of civil rights leader Dr. Martin Luther King Jr. on April 4, 1968. JOSEPH LOUW/TIME LIFE PICTURES/GETTY IMAGES

onto the balcony at 6:01. By 6:02, he was lying there with a bullet wound to his face.

After an international manhunt, an ex-convict drifter named James Earl Ray was arrested, and he confessed to the shooting. A 30.06 rifle was recovered in a doorway near the rooming house where he was staying, but a few days later, he recanted his confession and spent the rest of his life trying to prove his innocence.

There have been several re-openings of the case over the years, and the family of Martin Luther King Jr. is convinced that their patriarch was not taken down by Ray but by a conspiracy of government agencies. Although there has never been a clear enough trail of

Though born in Mississippi, yet another King, Riley "B. B." King made his name in Memphis, playing in clubs and working as a disc jockey at a local radio station.
Jim Luning

evidence to indict any person or agency, there are enough pieces to warrant suspicion.

It is a well-known fact that J. Edgar Hoover had been trying to gather evidence to discredit King for years, using illegal wiretaps and informants. The U.S. Army has since admitted it had up to 10 intelligence operatives monitoring the situation in Memphis and King's activities preceding his assassination. This was reportedly the same group that, in cooperation with the CIA, was running a little operation in Vietnam known as "Operation Phoenix," a systematic program to assassinate troublesome political leaders in that country. They used the offices of the Memphis Police Department for their operation.

When King was planning his "Poor People's March" in Washington, D.C., West Virginia Senator Robert Byrd proclaimed that King "must be stopped, before he creates another Memphis."

A report released by the U.S. Department of Justice in 2000 takes apart the conspiracy theory one line at a time, tossing off most of it as hearsay or noncredible testimony. Admittedly, some of the connections stretch thin, and many of the witnesses are dead or hard to take seriously. Still, one is left to wonder why, two years after the last investigation and trial and 32 years after King's murder, the federal government is still trying to convince people of its innocence.

The source of the black voice of the South for many years, the studios of WDIA are still located just off Beale Street in Memphis. JIM LUNING

Mayor of Beale Street: "Money talks, bullshit walks, and if you're broke, you're a joke."

When I drove through Las Vegas a few years ago, I was immediately struck by how petty the whole place seemed—the gilded playground of a petulant child, all polished steel and fake Venetian columns, reeking of a society with a short attention span. It was beautiful at night, of course, but for all the millions of light bulbs and dollars required to run them, I'd take a walk down Beale Street after a summer rain any night of the week.

The pavement looks dark and slick, and it picks up the color of the neon signs above. The street is almost empty. Between the rain, the ball game, and the fact it is a weeknight, the crowd is not what it could be. But loud music and boisterous voices issue from doorways and windows up and down the line.

B. B. King's place sits on the corner, and not far from that, at 126 Beale Street, is Elvis Presley's Memphis, a bar and restaurant operated by Elvis Presley Enterprises. Before being the Presley place, it was occupied by a men's clothing store called Lansky Brothers.

✦　✦　✦

He is the Clothier to the King, last of the true hep cats, and as much a part of Memphis history as Beale Street itself. Mr. Bernard Lansky (you will hear few people besides his son refer to him as anything else) speaks quickly, sprinkling sentences with hipster slang that comes out as a cross between cult jazz musician Slim Gaillard and the bandleader and comic Phil Harris. He is one of the few people that can use a phrase like "way out" and not sound like a Maynard G. Krebs wannabe.

These days, Mr. Bernard does business in the lobby of the Peabody Hotel, having moved over from his old location on Beale Street in the early 1980s. When you step into the shop, it takes a moment for you to decide if you have entered a men's clothing store or a guitar shop—hung on almost every wall, with room left for little else, are autographed guitars.

As of this writing, Mr. Bernard has been selling clothes in Memphis for 56 years and shows little sign of slowing down. Whether you're a visiting rock star or

Mr. Bernard J. Lansky, Clothier to the King and the mayor of Beale Street. His store now located in the Peabody Hotel, he leases out his old location, which is now "Elvis Presley's," a bar and restaurant operated by Elvis Presley Enterprises. Presley and many other famous performers shopped at Lansky's. Jim Luning

One of the landmarks on old Beale Street was Lansky Brothers, a clothing store catering to blues, rockabilly, and gospel performers. Bernard J. Lansky collection

a businessman passing through, he will take you through the store with a true love and enthusiasm for what he does.

When I asked him what he would suggest for an overgrown white boy whose summertime wardrobe runs to army surplus shorts and Hawaiian shirts, he gave me a look up and down and led me over to a couple of display racks.

"I think I'd put you onto some Tommy Bahama. That's the new silk look in pants," he said, stepping over to the next rack.

"Now looky here, man. This Nat Nash, a new line we just took on. Man, that stuff is blowin' outta here. We can't keep it. It's way out, high fashion."

Over the years, Mr. Bernard has outfitted some of the biggest names in show business, from rockabilly legends like Carl Perkins and Johnny Cash, to soul artists like Isaac Hayes. These days, the walls are covered with guitars signed by everyone from Dave Matthews to 311, and regardless of the style of music they play, if they are in Memphis, they come to see Mr. Bernard.

But why?

"People are always looking for something different, man," he explained. "They wanna be sharp, they want that up-to-date leisure look. What we have here at Lansky's is high-fashion merchandise.

"We opened in 1946, number 126 on famous Beale Street . . . *on famous Beale Street*," he added for emphasis.

"We had all the black entertainers, rhythm and blues, all the gospel singers . . . they all came to us."

And while he was taking care of the sartorial needs of the entertainers, Mr. Bernard occasionally noticed a skinny white kid peering in the windows. He was an usher at the local Loews movie theater.

"I didn't know who he was, so I invited him in to look around. After I showed him around and everything

A current selection of ties at Lansky's. Mr. Bernard specializes in "the up-to-date leisure look . . . high-fashion merchandise." JIM LUNING

Presley was an usher at the local movie theater when he first started stopping by to peer in the windows of Lansky Brothers. Mr. Bernard finally invited him in and showed him around. Eventually, Lansky fitted Presley throughout his early career in Memphis. The store often received mail from ardent fans, begging Lansky to pass along their notes to Elvis. BERNARD J. LANSKY COLLECTION

A selection of period advertising shows the modern look Lansky's specialized in. It's a shame that the Batman look never caught on. BERNARD J. LANSKY COLLECTION

it's a mod, mod, mod, mod, mod, world! at...

Lansky
BROTHERS

WHERE THE CARNABY LOOK IS IN!

Direct from Carnaby Street in London . . . The British Suit with the BOLERO look. Another in our "MOD" line that has created a sensation in Memphis and the Mid-South and all over the country. This suit is available in black, iridescent gold, iridescent blue-gold, and iridescent olive-gold.

● Mail Orders Filled Promptly

Carnaby Look at

Lansky
BROTHERS

THE YOUNG LONDON LOOK FROM CARNABY STREET IN LONDON

ANOTHER NEW SHIPMENT

Tom Jones Shirt

This Mod Shirt features a roll collar and full bloused effect. Assorted colors in solids and in large or medium polka dots. Sizes: X-Small, Small, Medium, Large and X-Large.

Bell Bottoms

Just Received a large shipment of all the latest styles, fabrics and colors.

HALCORD BELL
Available in white, burgundy or gold.

STRIPES
Comes in black & white, blue & gold, or red & white.

SUEDE
New in Burgundy, blue, olive or brown.

HERRINGBONE
In black and white only.

Shop Early While Selections are Complete

● Mail Orders Filled Promptly

LANSKY BROS., CORNER BEALE & SECOND STREETS

April 22, 1965

"HOLY RAVIOULI"

POW!

Lansky
BROTHERS

ZOT!

CRASH

Is where you'll find the...

BAT MAN SHIRT-JACKET

Pick up several in blue, purple, olive or black. The bat-cape is detachable and fully lined in a darker tone. Without the cape your shirt-jacket is a solid color with three-quarter length sleeves made for action living. Sizes small, medium and large. Be "boss" by being first to own the new Bat-Man shirt-jacket. ONLY 11.95!

MAIL ORDERS FILLED PROMPTLY
CORNER BEALE AND SECOND STS.

Sure We have the latest Mod Fashions, but we also have

CONTINENTAL STYLING

Lansky
BROTHERS

FOR YOUR CONVENIENCE

2-Button Continental Suit

Gentlemen . . . it's about time to switch to a totally new dimension in continental fashions. The formula . . . The Two Button Suit styled in imported worsteds (wool and mohair, wool and silk). Combine dramatic weaving, exact tailoring and the good taste of Lansky Brothers . . . The results: satisfaction, superb styling and the very newest dimension in continental styling. Semi-squared shoulders, side-vents, piped pockets and continental plain front trousers. Pin stripes, iridescents and solid colors.

Mail Orders Filled Promptly
CORNER of BEALE and SECOND STS.
FREE PARKING ONE DOOR WEST OF OUR STORE

he said, 'Look, man, I ain't got no money today, but when I get rich I'm gonna come back and buy you out.'

"I said, "Look here. Do me a favor, don't buy me out, just buy from me," Lansky recalled.

In time, the young usher found himself up on Union Street in a place run by a fellow named Sam Phillips. There, at Sun Studios, he strapped on a guitar and recorded a cover of a song by blues singer Arthur "Big Boy" Crudup. The song was "That's Alright Mama."

The usher, also known as Elvis Presley, was good to his word and came back to Mr. Bernard for some of that "high-fashion merchandise." Lansky fitted him for years.

Before he got into the clothing business, Lansky ran a small restaurant on Highway 61.

"We called it the Broken Drum . . . it can't be beat," he said with a laugh. "We used to have a dance band in there. We served sandwiches and cokes and ice. We had a nice crowd and did a very good business. That's when we were just kids and didn't know any better. We used to call that a 'Playhouse 90,' man . . . that's when you got nothing better to do.

"We used to go all the way down to Clarksdale all the time. This was way before I got married and everything. We used to go down there to see the girls . . . over 75 miles we'd drive just to get down there.

"The big thing down there at the time was the Holiday Inn, and then there was the Delta Tourist Court," he continued. "Then they had Isaqueena Street, which is like Beale Street here in Memphis. They had a theater down there, and all the Jewish merchants had dry goods stores along there."

But Mr. Bernard said he doesn't travel back down there that often anymore.

"Very seldom do I get down to the casinos any more. I haven't been down there in six months. I go down and eat and come back. I don't gamble, that's not my forté. They wanna give me a free meal? I'll buy my own meal."

When asked about current styles, Lansky just grinned and shook his head.

"Man . . . you don't fool with these guys. That's what you call a 'hip-hop look.' That never was our line. We're in fashion merchandise. That stuff is something new. It's an ugly look, a way-out look."

Beale Street, after a cooling summer rain. JIM LUNING

Highway 61 in Arkansas

Highway 61 sweeps south and west of downtown Memphis. To pick up 61 in Arkansas, it's a straight shot over the I-40 bridge. JIM LUNING

Thank God for Mississippi! That's the punch line to an old joke among politicians and educators from Arkansas when the subject of literacy rates and per capita incomes come up after a census.

While the two neighbors eternally duke it out over that coveted number-49 ranking, they have more in common than either wants to admit. Head far enough west in Arkansas and you're in the Ozarks. Head far enough east in Mississippi and you're in Hill Country. Clarksdale, Mississippi, is famous as a center of the blues, just like Helena, Arkansas, a few miles across the river.

On either side of the mighty river, slaves, then sharecroppers, scratched a living out of the rich loam of the upper Delta, harvesting cotton, rice, and catfish. While all those crops still pervade the area, the biggest harvest these days comes from the slot machines in Tunica and Robinsonville.

Cross the border from Missouri and you're greeted by a smaller version of the arch up in Saint Lou. Then there is a lot of nothing. Then there is Osceola.

The courthouse frames the town's square, and parked out front, you are sure that if you just wait there long enough, a lawyer in a white seersucker suit will emerge from the building, mopping his brow with a monogrammed handkerchief. It is the stuff of Faulkner and Grisham.

The remaining timbers of old slave quarters outside of Wilson, Arkansas, were photographed in 1941 as part of the Historic American Building Survey. LIBRARY OF CONGRESS

Frenchman's Bayou, Arkansas, sounded like a pretty good spot to stop for the night, so I called directory assistance looking for a hotel. The operator couldn't turn up any hotels—or any Frenchman's Bayou, for that matter. When I got to town, I understood why. JIM LUNING

Then you head south and there is more of nothing, save semis full of hogs on their way to becoming Tuesday lunches at The Rendezvous. Then there is West Memphis.

West Memphis is to Memphis as East Chicago, Indiana, is to the Windy City—a boil on the ass. It adds nothing but gas stations and chain motels; it returns nothing but diesel smoke and the odor of pig shit. Forever staring across the Mississippi River, like the ne'er-do-well younger brother of a local hero, it is Purgatory.

Downtown Osceola, the seat of Mississippi County, Arkansas. Most of the short stretch of Highway 61 that passes through Arkansas is within the county. JIM LUNING

Then and now. A welcome arch over Highway 61, at the Arkansas–Missouri border, photographed in July 1950. MISSOURI DEPARTMENT OF TRANSPORTATION ARCHIVES. *The same arch today, the spot where the gas station once stood is now a favorite spot for truckers to drop trailers.* KIP WELBORN

Lambert's Café: "Just throw the damned thing!"

When you pick up the menu, it takes a moment to register the fact that it is actually a menu and not a laminated script page from an old episode of *Hee Haw:* "Hog jowls and collard greens, ham and cornbread, termaters n' onions. And rolls. Lord, yes, there are rolls. And sweet tea to float a navy."

There is dining, and there is cuisine. There are cafés and patisseries and trattorias. *This* is eatin'.

You would think that by three o'clock in the afternoon, most restaurants would be past their lunch rush, yet as I turned off 61 in Sikeston, Missouri, and headed for Lambert's Café, I noticed the line of people waiting to get in before I ever saw the sign. The wait for a table was running 45 minutes to an hour.

Inside it's a hectic scene, with people waddling toward the exit packed to the gills and others coming to take a recently vacated booth. In between, a small crew of bussers approaches the booth and, in something akin to a pit stop at Indy, they strip, clean, and reset the service in just a few seconds. It's a far cry from 1942, when Earl and Agnes Lambert opened an eight-table, nine-stool café on South Main.

It's been famous in the area for decades, and once Interstate 55 came through, Lambert's was guaranteed more business. They've opened two other locations in addition to their Sikeston home. JIM LUNING

Behind every cart of rolls at Lambert's is another waiter with a big can of sorghum molasses to put on the rolls. Lambert's also sells cans to go in their gift shop. JIM LUNING

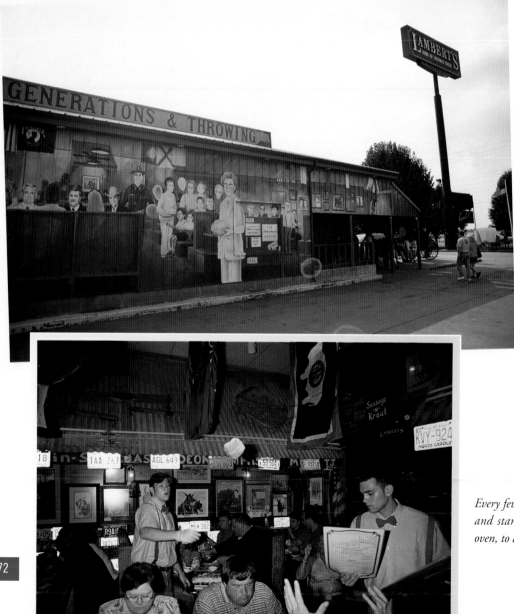

Every few minutes, a server comes out of the kitchen and starts throwing rolls, hot and fresh from the oven, to anyone who raises a hand. JIM LUNING

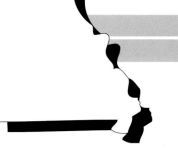

Both Agnes and Earl originally hailed from Winfield, Alabama. In 1924 Earl Lambert was 24 years old and owned a fledgling house-moving business. Well, what he really had was a secondhand tractor, but it worked well enough to pull a house a ways. In late September 1924, he was contracted to move a house for one Mr. Dyer of Winfield.

Earl showed up on the appointed day and began slowly towing the home to its new location. But in the middle of town, right in front of the drugstore, his tractor broke down. Traffic was blocked, and the family was stranded. He contacted the widow in Texas from whom he had bought the tractor to ask where her husband had bought spare parts.

On October 1, 1924, Lambert frantically cabled the Farmer's Friend Tractor Company in Earthworm City, Illinois, describing the "big bull gear" in the back that needed replacement.

This spectacular view looks down into a valley of corn and wheat fields, 561 feet above sea level, along Highway 61 in southern Missouri. JIM LUNING

The company sent him back a lovely letter asking him to consult the parts catalog they had enclosed so they could know the proper part number. Lambert wrote back, saying he couldn't find the part number, mostly because they had not sent him any damned catalog.

The company responded immediately, apologizing for the error, and sent him a parts catalog. The only hitch was, since most of that particular model run had been sold to the French to pull artillery in World War I, they didn't have any English catalogs, just French.

Lambert wrote back, thanking them for the catalog, but explaining, "I can't understand the dago printing . . . the pictures don't look like anything I have ever seen before. It's the one with 44 teeth that meshes into the one with 12 teeth. Send it right away!"

The Farmer's Friend Tractor Company of Earthworm City, Illinois, wrote back dutifully, explaining that his particular model came with a 45-tooth gear, not a 44-tooth one. They shipped him a 45-tooth model. In the meantime, the house had been sitting in downtown Winfield, blocking traffic for three weeks. Lambert wrote back again, pleading:

Old man Dyer says if I don't get some action for him soon, he is going to hire horses and move it himself, and if I expect to see a cent I can just sue him. The police department has served me notice I have until next Thursday to move the house or get pinched. Plus Mr. Dyer said today he hoped I wasn't still thinking of getting married, and I expect he may have some say in the matter, owing to the fact that the girl I expect to marry is named Agnes Dyer and is unfortunately the daughter of Old Mr. Dyer.

The floodwall at Cape Girardeau makes a fine canvas for murals (below left). In addition to the riverfront, murals can be found at many other locations throughout town. The opposite side of the floodwall (below) bears the years and levels to which the Mississippi River has flooded over the years. JIM LUNING

In desperation, Lambert sent them the broken gear and asked them to send another one "just like it, but without 6 teeth busted out." But Old Mr. Dyer had grown tired of waiting, and on October 31, 1924, he assembled teams of horses and an old flivver to tow his house. But when Dyer gave the command to start pulling, the starting car spooked the horses, which gave a sudden jerk, causing the timbers to slip and the kitchen addition to slowly crack and fall off the side of the house into the street. Dyer, furious, forbade the marriage, and Lambert was sunk.

But, as it turned out, the Farmer's Friend Tractor Company had just sold one of their tractors to a farmer up the rail line. They dispatched a service man to go to the farm, get the tractor, and drive it to Winfield to help Lambert. He arrived on November 7 and moved the house to its new location with ease. Then he telegraphed his report to the main office.

The serviceman, Luke Torkle, explained that the night before, Lambert had sold everything he owned (a secondhand tractor, a radio set, and the house-moving business) for $450 and taken the train north with a girl named Agnes Dyer, saying that they were to be married and live in Missouri. He had told people he had no idea what sort of business he would get into, but that it would not involve machinery or house moving in any way.

Torkle also managed to take a look at Lambert's tractor and realized why they had such a tough time getting the proper part for it. "It's not one of ours," he reported. "It's a 1920 model from the SE Tractor Company of Philadelphia." Apparently the widow from whom Lambert bought the tractor had confused it with a different one her husband owned and gave him the wrong parts information.

Earl and Agnes settled outside Sikeston and began sharecropping—using mules—and working at a shoe factory before opening the first Lambert's Café in 1942. Agnes didn't return to see her family for three years. Earl never set foot in Winfield, Alabama, again.

✦   ✦   ✦

A slight clash of technologies photographed on Highway 61 in October 1951, as a horse-drawn wagon holds up traffic south of Cape Girardeau, up 61 a piece from Sikeston. MISSOURI DEPARTMENT OF TRANSPORTATION ARCHIVES

Its rails long cold and its doors long shuttered, an abandoned factory lines the roadway north of Cape Girardeau. JIM LUNING

What happens once you're seated can best be described as a feeding frenzy. No matter what you order, a steady stream of free side dishes is constantly loaded onto your plate. It is loud and hectic, disorganized and delicious. It seems every high school kid in the county must work here, bussing tables, dishing sides, or throwing rolls.

That last tradition is said to have begun in the 1970s, when an impatient customer couldn't wait any longer for a roll and finally yelled to the waitress, "Just throw the damned thing!" Lambert's became "home of the throwed rolls." They have been featured on everything from Letterman and Leno, to *That's Incredible* and *The Simpsons*. Although the gimmick may get them the odd customer, it is the food that brings them back in droves.

Lambert's ovens run almost nonstop, averaging 520 dozen rolls each day. The rolls are 5 inches across, and managers figure that in the last two years they have made enough to reach Memphis.

In the last year, they fried just over a quarter-million pounds of chicken (livers included) and 132,000 pounds of beef (256 choice steers' worth). They've fried more than 70,000 pork chops, and on average, serve up about 400 pounds of hog jowls each week. It is reportedly bet-ter than bacon. I don't have the heart to try them.

When your order arrives, someone also wheels by with a huge bowl of fried okra, or tomatoes and onions, or macaroni salad or slaw—this is all free, mind you—in addition to whatever you order, refilling your plate at the drop of a my-mouth's-too-full-to-talk-but-lay-it-on-me-anyway-sport nod and grunt.

Every other minute, the president of the local FFA chapter bursts out of the kitchen door and yells, "Rolls!" Then the hands start shooting up, and a few seconds later, the same scene plays out booth by booth.

Someone catches a roll, mutters "Ow!" and tosses it into the other hand. At this point he or she says, "Jesus," and toss it back into the first hand. The level of profanity to follow is predicated mostly on the temperature of the roll and the number of times the person keeps tossing it from hand to hand before he or she finally figures it out and puts the thing on the plate. Comic opera . . . with catering.

Following the old road north through Cape Girardeau County, Missouri, near Fruitland, just one portion of 61's length that comprises part of the "Great River Road." Jim Luning

Chuck Berry: Modern Prometheus

> *Chorus: And have frail mortals now the flame-bright fire"*
> *Prometheus: Yea, and shall master many arts thereby.*
>
> —*Aeschylus*, Prometheus Bound

Being a speculative look toward future inter-galactic relations.

On a distant planet sometime in the future, there are two young aliens looking over the remains of a primitive space probe they've found. Inside, it has pictures of earthlings on it and some sort of prehistoric data storage device called a long-playing record. After a sympathetic greeting from a Nazi war criminal, there are examples of what the earthlings call music.

As the aliens sample the different sounds sent from Earth, they come across something almost indescribable. It starts off with some sort of amplified vibrations, then some pounding noises. After a bit of this, there is a type of singing. The words sound like . . .

"Deep down in Louisiana close to New Orleans. . . ."

Apparently, it is an exhortation for someone to leave the area, as the singer keeps telling a creature named Johnny to "go." The aliens are enamored of this strange sound and increase the volume fivefold. As they listen over and over, they consider adopting alternate hairstyles and wearing tight trousers. Further examination of the probe is curtailed, as one of the alien's parents enters the room and orders them to turn that damned noise down.

◆ ◆ ◆

Charles Edward Anderson Berry was born in St. Louis, Missouri, on October 18, 1926, the third of six kids by Henry and Martha Berry, a contractor and school-teacher, respectively. He grew up at 2520 Goode Avenue in a section of St. Louis known as "The Ville." It was a prosperous area for local blacks, where they could own property and do business with little harassment.

Berry attended Sumner High School, where in 1941, he made his first public performance of note, performing Jay McShann's "Confessin' the Blues" at a school talent show. Sumner was

The man who invented rock n' roll, Chuck Berry, still regularly performs in St. Louis and jets around the country playing oldies shows. He lives just outside St. Louis, in Ladue, Missouri. AUTHOR COLLECTION

The old Anheuser-Busch brewery in St Louis, Missouri—responsible for hundreds of jobs, millions of hangovers, and, no doubt, at least a few thousand unintended children. LIBRARY OF CONGRESS

Flowering bushes still line Highway 61 in Missouri during high summer. This photograph was made in August 1950. MISSOURI DEPARTMENT OF TRANSPORTATION ARCHIVES

Finnish architect EeroSaarinen designed the stainless steel Gateway Arch for a 1947 competition soliciting an appropriate memorial to westward expansion. The structure, which at 630 feet is the tallest memorial in the United States, was built between 1961 and 1966. CATHY MORRISON, MISSOURI DEPARTMENT OF TRANSPORTATION

The 12-inch, gold-plated copper record Sounds of Earth *aboard the space probe* Voyager 1 *contains greetings in 55 languages and samples of music from different cultures and eras—including Chuck Berry's "Johnny B. Goode." The gold aluminum cover was designed to protect the record from micrometeorite bombardment, but also provides the finder a key to playing the record. The explanatory diagram was etched on both the inner and outer surfaces of the cover because the outer diagram was expected to erode in time.* National Aeronautics and Space Administration

the first black high school west of the Mississippi, and other alumni include Dick Gregory, Arthur Ashe, Tina Turner, and Robert Guillaume. But Berry wasn't destined for a cap and gown.

While taking a joyride to Kansas City, Berry and a few friends were arrested and charged with armed robbery. It earned the budding guitarist a 10-year sentence. He was released on his twenty-first birthday in 1947.

He bounced from job to job, sometimes working with his father, sometimes in the local Fischer auto body plant, and all the while playing guitar on the side.

By New Year's 1952, Berry was asked to join Sir John's Trio, a popular local group with drummer Ebby Hardy and pianist Johnnie Johnson. Berry's electric guitar and onstage energy added immensely to the band's popularity, and soon Berry was leading the band.

In 1955, Berry contacted Chess Records, whose house producer at the time, none other than Willie Dixon, loved Berry's version of "Ida Red,"

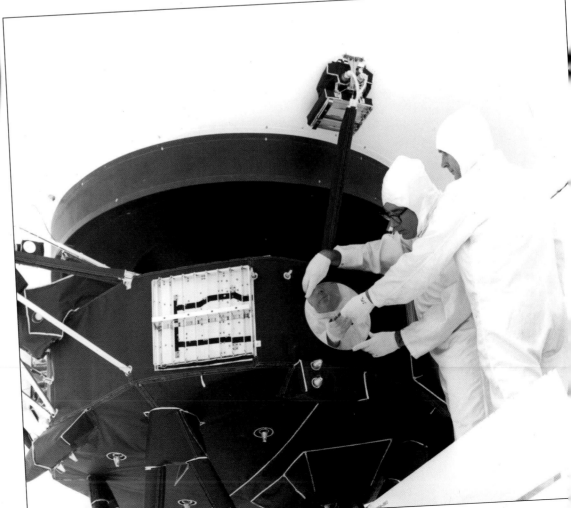

A gold-plated record with Sounds of Earth *is mounted to its flight bracket on the mission module of the* Voyager 1 *spacecraft.* National Aeronautics and Space Administration

an old, western-swing fiddle tune he reworked as a rock rave-up. Dixon called Berry's band to Chicago and they cut the song and changed its name to "Maybelline." Cleveland disc jockey Alan Freed played it for two hours straight when he got his copy. The rest is history.

In exchange for playing the record, Freed swung a deal that registered himself and a friend as co-writers along with Berry, cutting Berry's royalties by two-thirds in the process. Berry also learned that his manager had been pocketing money from his live performances. Regardless, Berry prospered and bought a parcel of land near Wentzville, Missouri, and opened a nightclub called Club Bandstand near the theater district.

In 1959, Berry met a girl in Yuma, Arizona, and hired her to work as a coat checker at Club Bandstand. Unfortunately, she didn't work out and was fired a few weeks later. With nowhere to go, she tried hooking in a local hotel for a few days before giving up and calling the police back in Yuma, asking how she could get home.

As the story unfolded, most of the details were obscured save two: Chuck Berry and prostitution. Berry was charged with violating the Mann Act—transporting a woman across state lines for immoral purposes.

His first trial was eventually thrown out after the judge became belligerent and hurled racial insults at Berry. He was found guilty at the second trial and sentenced to three years in jail. He went into prison in February 1962. It was a potentially career-ending scandal, but by the time he was released on parole in October 1963, his career was flourishing.

The Rolling Stones released their versions of "Come On," "Carol," and "You Can't Catch Me," while the Beatles covered "Rock and Roll Music," and "Roll Over Beethoven." The Beach Boys took liberties with Berry's "Sweet Little Sixteen," turning it into "Surfin' U.S.A."

He came back with a vengeance, releasing six singles in just over a year. But by 1966 his string of hits had run out and styles were changing. Berry left Chess for Mercury Records and recorded a string of watered-down new records and money-grabbing remakes of his older hits.

With a recording of Chuck Berry's "Johnny B. Goode" aboard, VOYAGER 1 *lifts off on September 5, 1977, on a mission to the outer planets.* NATIONAL AERONAUTICS AND SPACE ADMINISTRATION

In 1972, he re-signed with Chess and released his first number-one record, a remake of a song he had done on a live record four years earlier called "My Tambourine." This time, Berry called it "My Ding-a-Ling."

It was a ridiculous, but catchy ditty, the kind of song your grandmother could hum along with, yet never realize what the words were about. That first number-one must have felt good to Berry, who had been slogging away for 20 years in the business. But if there was icing on that particular cake, it was that the song Berry blocked from the top of the charts was the latest from Elvis, "Burning Love."

❖   ❖   ❖

When the Voyager probes were launched in 1977, they contained drawings of humans, a chart showing our place in the solar system, and a record titled *Sounds of Earth,* a collection of sounds heard on, well, Earth. On the record, people say, "hello" in 55 different languages, but most of what is included is music, from Navajo chanting, to ragas, to Bulgarian folk songs. There is a representative collection of classical music and, of all things, Berry's original recording of "Johnny B. Goode."

All these pieces—assuming that advanced extraterrestrial societies exist and use turntables—are our attempt to explain ourselves, to justify our existence, and extend a hand of friendship across the galaxy. There may be no telling what sort of job we've done, even if something finds a probe, but we could do worse than to send them Chuck Berry records.

These days, Berry lives outside St. Louis in Ladue. He still performs regularly, up to 80 shows a year, and requires exactly three things when you book him: a Lincoln Town Car waiting for him at the airport, an amplifier, and a backup band. While most musicians are meticulous about preparing for shows, there is no rehearsal when Berry arrives at the venue, sometimes not even a sound check. It's up to local promoters to find a band to back him, and they never have to look far. Anyone with an electric guitar probably learned half the Berry catalog before building up the nerve to come out of the garage with the thing. Sometimes the bands are a bit lacking, but Berry soldiers on, either ignoring their mistakes or pushing them to keep up with him . . . usually both.

If there were justice in the world, the U.S. Patent Office would have registered Berry as the inventor of rock n' roll years ago. He is sometimes disappointed that the crowds only want to hear his oldies, but such has grown to be his lot in life and place in history. Having discovered fire itself, it's hard to get folks to look at the new butane lighter you've come up with.

A cartoon likeness of Big Mama, the proprietor of Shorty's Bar and Grill in New London.

A mural on the side of a boarded-up used furniture store welcomes travelers to the town of New London, Misouri, north of St. Louis.

Inter. U.S. 66 & 61   St. Louis Co.   Mo.   Oct. '48

Route 66 passed over Highway 61 on the western edge of St. Louis. MISSOURI DEPARTMENT OF TRANSPORTATION ARCHIVES. *The decorative bridge photographed in October 1948 is now a thing of the past, replaced by a typical modern concrete overpass.*

81

Brian Henneman: Tunes from All Three Hanks

He has a permanent grin, the sort a fellow might give you when he knows you're about to sit on a whoopee cushion and the anticipation is just killing him. At an outdoor table behind Frederick's Musical Inn on old Route 66 in St. Louis, Brian Henneman and his band mates are relaxing with beers as the opening act begins their set. The band that started out as a summer side project the year before is still going strong.

Henneman, best known as the lead singer and guitarist of the Bottle Rockets, is playing in Diesel Island (think truck stop, not palm trees) with Rockets drummer Mark Ortmann, and John Horton on bass and Kip Loui on vocals and acoustic guitar. Simply put, these are men with sideburns.

"We're doing an '81 Conway tonight," said Henneman grinning, as if recommending a fine wine. "And we play tunes from all three Hanks," indicating the Williams Sr., Jr., and III.

✦   ✦   ✦

Brian Henneman grew up in Festus, Missouri, on Highway 61 and worked as a guitar tech for the band Uncle Tupelo before getting a record contract of his own and fronting The Bottle Rockets. Henneman's trademark twang comes courtesy of a Fender Telecaster and a Peavey amplifier. Like many country guitarists, Henneman uses a pick AND fingers to produced pedal steel bends.

In the mid-1990s, when bands like Pearl Jam were moping their way around a fading grunge scene, the Bottle Rockets were quickly gaining notice around their Missouri home base. Their first album was well received, but it would be their second, *The Brooklyn Side,* that hit the play lists of Americana radio stations. It has been described as "a day in the life of Festus," that being their hometown of Festus, Missouri, located alongside Highway 61. So it may come as something of a scandal to discover that Henneman, pride of Festus, was actually born in Crystal City.

"The hospital was right at the intersection of Highway 61 and 67," he ex-plained. "I think later that Festus annexed that corner or something, but at the time it was officially Crystal City.

"It was the highway to everything," Henneman said with a laugh, recalling his first memories of Highway 61. "It was the only way to go. By time I got older, I-55 came through, but when I was a little kid [Highway 61] just sort of stopped there in Festus. When I was a kid, there used to be this big hole down on the south end of town, and there was this old fireworks stand down there. That used to be the big thing when I was little. My dad would stick me in the car and we would go down and buy fireworks."

Hence the Bottle Rockets' moniker.

It was a typical small-town childhood, according to Henneman. Growing up, the main form of entertainment for teens was driving up and down the main drag for hours. Then, a McDonald's opened up on Highway 61, and all was well with the adolescent world. But Henneman and his friends didn't spend a lot of time doing the circuit.

"We didn't really have a regular spot we hung out at," he recalled. "We were kind of like the weirdoes in town. We never really got into the hanging-out scene. There was this one place right down on Highway 61 called Crystal Donut. That's where all the cool dope-smoking dudes would hang out."

"Actually it was a combination donut shop and pool hall," Ortmann interjected from across the table. "In fact, the first bar we ever played in, was this place called

By the end of the night, even the metalheads are pumping their fists in the air along with Henneman (in hat) and his side project, Diesel Island. Though sometimes performed tongue-in-cheek, the band's repertoire reprises classic country from the 1960s and 1970s.

the Hi-Point. That was on 61, too. Our first gig there was like '86 or '87 or something."

"That was a band called Chicken Truck, which is not that different than what we are doing here with Diesel Island," added Henneman. "We were playing a lot of songs that we thought were cool, but we sucked. Actually, we didn't suck; we were great. It's just the people all wanted to hear the latest pop-country song, and we weren't into that."

Around the same time, just across the Mississippi in Belleville, Illinois, Jeff Tweedy and Jay Farrar, along with drummer Mike Heidorn, had formed Uncle Tupelo. Henneman eventually went on tour with them as a guitar tech and occasionally sat in during shows on old country covers.

"They were recording songs for their second album, and I would just go along with them, and we would fool around with this new DAT [Digital Audio Tape] machine. We goofed off and did a couple songs I had written," he explained.

"So I am out on tour with them, and their manager started passing around this demo I had done and got me a record deal. I was like, 'What the fuck? I don't even have a band!'"

That was then; this is now.

✦ ✦ ✦

Later that night, Kip Loui steps up to the microphone with a pained look and says flatly, "This is gonna be horrible." A second later Brian Henneman plays the intro to Glen Campbell's disco-country mishmash, "Southern Nights." The crowd, a youngish bunch wearing an inordinate number of heavy-metal T-shirts, begins hooting wildly.

For the next hour or two, Diesel Island culls the pop-country songbook, playing the classic and questionable with equal gusto. From George Strait, to John Anderson, to all three Hanks, the sound is rooted in Henneman's Telecaster-via-Peavey twang.

By the end of the evening, people are pumping their fists in the air to "Louisiana Saturday Night," sloshing ice-cold Stag beer into the air with each thrust. Eyeing the clock, Henneman announces the last song and last call.

As the last notes echo throughout the basement club, a few well-wishers stop and chat with band members. Ortmann tears down his drum kit quickly, carefully packing away the toms and cymbals. Horton winds his bass cord around his arm as Kip Loui snaps shut his case. The house policy of not paying the band until the equipment is out the door is not far from anyone's mind.

HABS No. MO-1619-1

The old post office in Ste. Genevieve, Missouri, the oldest French settlement west of the Mississippi River. Ste. Genevieve is south of Festus and was immortalized in song by Henneman's friend, Jay Farrar. LIBRARY OF CONGRESS

Singer-songwriter Jay Farrar grew up across the Mississippi River from Highway 61 in Belleville, Illinois. He wrote many of the songs on the album TRACE, *recorded with his former band Son Volt, while driving 61 between New Orleans and St. Paul, Minnesota.* JIM NEWBERRY

Jay Farrar: "On and On That Road Winds"

Jay Farrar formed Uncle Tupelo with his schoolmate, Jeff Tweedy, right across the river from Festus, Missouri, in Belleville, Illinois. After the band broke up in 1994, Tweedy went on to form Wilco, while Farrar founded Son Volt, which he has since put on "extended hiatus."

"I spent a lot of hours driving Highway 61 south to north and back again," Farrar says. "Highway 61 was the backdrop as I made several trips from New Orleans to Minneapolis in 1995 while writing songs and rehearsing for the Son Volt *Trace* album.

"I think of Highway 61 in three parts. The southern section connecting Memphis to New Orleans is a pulsating entity like an artery for the Mississippi Delta blues. The middle section became familiar to me as I made drives from my home base in St. Louis north to Iowa City to play shows, south to hang out with the Bottle Rockets in Festus, and sometimes farther down to the oldest French settlement west of the Mississippi, in St. Genevieve. The northern part belongs to Bob Dylan: 'We'll put some bleachers out in the sun and have it all out on Highway 61.'"

Hannibal, Missouri: The Huck Stops Here

It was a drizzly Sunday morning, and up and down the streets of Hannibal were white tents full of local artists, crafters, and foodies who watch the sky with dread. In the three or four blocks, there were maybe 100 people milling about, browsing their way down one side and back up the other.

Having a famous son must be a mixed blessing for a town like Hannibal. Although Mark Twain put Hannibal on the map and guaranteed it a certain tourist base, being so invested in a single story must get tiring. While there are the bona fide historical spots where the author had actually lived and worked, the Twain name is everywhere, from steamboats, to beer distributorships, to state parks.

Mark Twain, or Sam Clemens as he was known then, was born November 30, 1835, in Florida, Missouri. When he was four, his family moved 30 miles east to the riverfront town of Hannibal. Roaming the bluffs and caves above town, Clemens laid the groundwork for his greatest novel, *Huckleberry Finn*.

He has been called the greatest American writer, and more flattering, the *first* American writer. Although he would likely be embarrassed, and possibly disgusted, by the way his name and life have been turned into marketing engines, the town of Hannibal is probably the only tourist attraction that one needs to read great American novels to fully appreciate.

At one end of downtown sits Cardiff Hill, the playground for Huck, Tom, and Twain himself. Atop it is the Twain Lighthouse, which, according to tourism folks, is the largest inland lighthouse in the country. At the base of the hill is the famous statue of Twain's childhood *doppelgangers,* and just behind is the long, steep stairwell to the top. It's typical for visitors to stroll the historic district and then take the stairs up the hill for the scenic view. It's also typical for them to begin regretting that decision about halfway up. I did, and I did.

But regardless of the wheezing and wobbly legs, once you reach the top the view is worth it. From Cardiff Hill, all of Hannibal lies before you. If you make the extra trek up the lighthouse, there are views of the Mississippi as it might have looked in Twain's youth.

Twain was a prolific writer, turning his boyhood adventures into novels and cranking out historical fiction, moralistic fables, and dark fantasy. In his early days, he was a newspaper correspondent, filing florid, if not always factual, reports from the West. Yet to get to the essence of Twain's acerbic wit, it's better to look beyond the published classics and to the various letters, speeches, and assorted tirades that he penned over the years instead. Written as letters to the editor, recited at dinner events with cigar in hand, or drafted as tongue-in-cheek petitions to foreign heads of state, they show the author's beloved crankiness in a clearer light.

It was while roaming the bluffs and caves around Hannibal as a youngster that Mark Twain, then known as Samuel Clemens, laid the groundwork for some of his greatest writing. MARK TWAIN MUSEUM

> *"The Mississippi River will always have its own way; no engineering skill can persuade it to do otherwise. . ."*
>
> —*Mark Twain*

At a dinner in Paris in 1879, Twain, in a hilarious turn, rose to deliver "Some Thoughts on the Science of Onanism." Starting with Homer and working in the Pope, the Queen of England, and Brigham Young along the way, he puts the ancient art in historical perspective. Also, he offers tips to spot the "signs of excessive indulgence in this destructive pastime," listing them thusly: "a disposition to eat, to drink, to smoke, to meet together convivially, to laugh, to tell indelicate stories—and mainly, a yearning to paint pictures."

✦   ✦   ✦

The annual Mark Twain Days festival, held over the Fourth of July, is pure, if predictable, Americana. There are Tom and Becky look-alike contests, a fence-painting competition, and, of course, a frog-jumping contest. In between, Twain impersonators recite from different books, usually at the Mark Twain Hotel. Up and down the main drag of Hannibal, hundreds of local artists and hawkers line the street, peddling small pieces of an unrelated dream. While it's usually good karma to stimulate the local economy along the way, perhaps the finest tribute you could pay to the man behind the town is to (re)read his work.

Samuel Clemens, or Mark Twain as he came to be known, was actually born 30 miles away, in Florida, Missouri, but he grew up in Hannibal. Hannibal Convention & Visitors Bureau

A statue of Mark Twain's most famous characters, Tom Sawyer and Huckleberry Finn, stands at the bottom of Cardiff Hill.

The Mississippi River as Twain might have seen it. High atop the lighthouse on Cardiff Hill, you can look out over the river without seeing the town below.

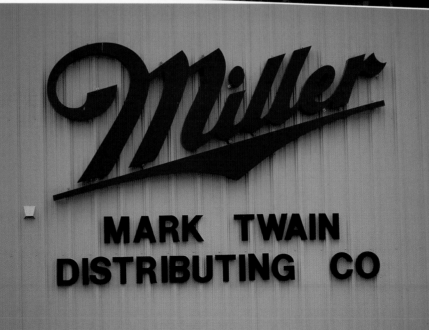

Twain's name is plastered on just about every sort of business in the Hannibal area. Troops from the Miller Brewing Company in Milwaukee made it as far south as Hannibal, before being turned back by Budweiser loyalists, mustered in from St. Louis.

Looking down over the historic town of Hannibal, Missouri, from the top of Cardiff Hill, where Mark Twain—then Samuel Clemens—played as a boy.

The Mark Twain Hotel, located next to the river, closed for business decades ago but is still used for receptions and theater events and is available for rent, lease, or sale.

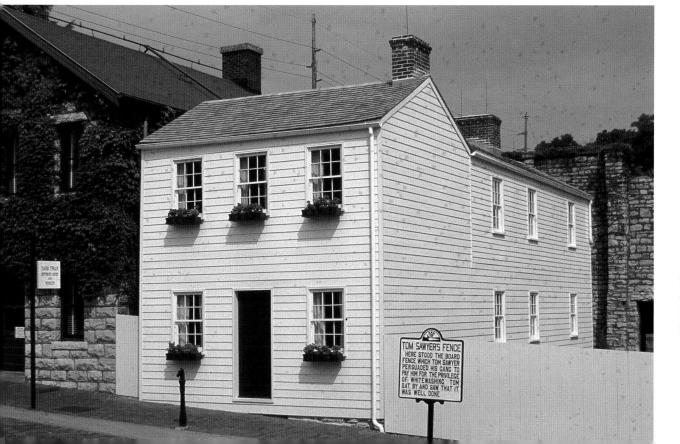

Twain's boyhood home, now preserved as a museum, is one of the many Twain-related locations tourists come to Hannibal to visit. HANNIBAL CONVENTION & VISITORS BUREAU

Canton: "God Blessed our Town"

The drizzle in Hannibal gave way to sheets of rain north of Palmyra. I was headed for Canton, home to the country's oldest continuously operating ferry across the Mississippi. On the edge of town, there was what looked to be an almost completed motel, and across the road the remnants of a trailer in the process of being bulldozed. I turned right and headed into the business district.

Given it was early Sunday afternoon, most of the shops in town were closed. But there was a light on at the Hat Rack Café, and a few minutes later, I was sitting down with a hot cup of coffee. The place was mostly deserted—one other table waited for their check—and after they left, I struck up a conversation with the waitress.

I mentioned it looked like they had a new motel going in on the edge of town, and she gave me a bit of an odd look. When I said it looked like a tornado had hit the place across the road from it, she cocked her head again and said, "One did."

I rolled into Canton on May 30. Twenty days before, a cluster of tornadoes sped across western Illinois and northeastern Missouri. As the waitress began telling me about that day, I vaguely remembered a brief story I had heard on National Public Radio weeks before.

I finished my coffee and followed the directions she gave to the area she described as being hit the worst. The lighted sign outside the café's front door read, "God Blessed our Town. Happy Memorial Day." The path of the tornado started near Culver Stockton College, where it tore off a roof and continued west, hitting more than 70 homes before exiting the other side of town.

I smelled the sawdust before I realized I was at my turn off. At just about every other house, carpenters were busily replacing damaged sections of the houses' roofs, rebuilding porches, and hauling away debris. Heading west through town, the neighborhood changed. The huge Victorians on the main drag gave way to smaller ranches and Cape Cods, which sat unrepaired. It was a combat zone.

The tornado seemed to have skipped back and forth across the street, snapping its tail like an angry alligator. One house was simply gone, nothing but the foundation remaining, while right next door the satellite TV dish bolted to the front railing was not even bent.

Up and down the street, the damaged homes bore messages in fluorescent orange spray paint that indicated whether they were safe or too structurally damaged to inhabit. I stopped to take a closer look at some of the buildings as the whine of power saws echoed across the neighborhood.

Driving through the town of Canton, Missouri, one Sunday morning, I was left to wonder why the phrase "act of God" almost always describes large-scale destruction and the death of innocent people.

I walked around a two-block area, drawing the odd stare from residents in various stages of cleanup. The drizzle changed to rain, and after shooting a few pictures, I made my way back to where I had parked. I started the van, turned on the windshield wipers, and was about to pull out when I saw something across the street. There stood a man, apparently oblivious to the rain that was now pounding down, washing his SUV. Behind him, his house was missing most of its windows and about half of its roof, which was covered with a huge blue tarp. What was once the garage was now a pile of building materials in his backyard. But the SUV was spotless, nary a ding or streak of mud to be seen. He continued spraying it with a hose, as rain ran down his forehead and into his eyes.

His face was screwed up into a sort of deadpan squint, giving no clue as to what he might have been thinking. Did he realize the dumb irony of the scene, washing his car in the rain as his house sat ruined behind him? Probably not. Probably for the first time in weeks, though, he was able to ignore the flattened neighborhood around him and the leaking roof behind him, and concentrate on one simple, undamaged, normal thing.

> *"Another road remains,*
> *but it provides no more.*
> *It can only take us away.*
> *Southbound, you can taste the weather,*
> *It feels like home."*
>
> —*Jay Farrar, "Route"*

A memorial to the Confederate dead stands outside the Marion County, Missouri, courthouse.

The oldest continuously operating ferry across the upper Mississippi still runs to from Canton, Missouri, to Illinois near Lock and Dam 20.

Fort Madison: Burning Down the House

In 1965, outside of the Shaeffer Pen Company in downtown Fort Madison, someone noticed something odd poking through the parking lot. Excavations of the site by the Iowa state archeologist revealed the ruins of old Fort Madison, which burned to the ground in 1813.

When the town of Fort Madison was re-settled in 1833, all that remained of the old structure were a few crumbling cellar walls. In time most of those were gone as well. Little thought was paid to the original site as the city developed.

Town fathers had entertained proposals for rebuilding the fort since the 1930s, but it wasn't until 1983, when the city received grant money from the Iowa Historical Society, that construction began. Replica buildings were erected out of large oak timbers, shaped and fitted by inmate volunteers working at the nearby Iowa State Penitentiary. Once assembled and checked at the prison, the buildings were taken apart, shipped to Fort Madison, then reassembled in Riverview Park.

◆　◆　◆

Forty-four soldiers from the First Infantry began construction of the fort in 1808. Their commander, Lieutenant Alpha Kingsley, christened the outpost Fort Madison in honor of President James Madison. While it was indeed a U.S. military installation—the first on the upper Mississippi, in fact—its real function was more Wal-Mart than warfare.

What the soldiers were charged with guarding was the post "factory," where Native Americans came to trade furs for manufactured goods, such as fishhooks, blankets, traps, and knives. Although most of the surrounding tribes coexisted with the post, roaming

The state of Iowa, sometimes laughingly referred to as "The Gateway to Nebraska," promises "Fields of Opportunity," an allusion to the oceans of corn the state produces.

Fort Madison itself was reconstructed by city fathers with help from federal funding.

bands of Winnebago, Seaquake, and Sauk warriors often harassed the settlement.

In 1810, Kingsley ordered a "tail" section added to the compound to defend against arrows and musket fire from the rear. Two years later, during the War of 1812, Sauk warriors and their allies attacked the post again, killing a soldier they captured outside the walls, burning cabins, and slaughtering the cattle tended by the soldiers.

Under siege, the factory was purposely burned to prevent the attacking Sauks from doing so on a day when west winds would drive the embers into the rest of the post. Later that month, a detachment of 19 soldiers from Fort Belle Fontaine in St. Louis was sent north to reinforce the beleaguered troops. They stopped in Hannibal and picked up a small squad of U.S. Rangers, whose commanding officer was Captain Nathan Boone, son of frontiersman Daniel Boone.

The soldiers made it through that winter and on into the summer of 1813. In July, two men out cutting timber for a new blockhouse were found dead, and a week later four Rangers were also killed. All through August the post endured barrages of flaming arrows. Finally, that September, new post commander Lieutenant Thomas Hamilton ordered Fort Madison abandoned. The remaining troops set fire to the buildings and floated down river in the ensuing confusion.

During the summer tourist season, the city of Fort Madison hires local students to portray soldiers and their wives and perform "living history" demonstrations.

The interior of the reconstructed fort features typical officers' quarters during the heyday of America's westward expansion. Enlisted men lived in bunkhouse-style rooms.

✦ ✦ ✦

One hundred ninety years later, the reconstructed Fort Madison is the centerpiece of Riverview Park, flanked by a riverboat casino to the south and manicured grounds to the north. You enter the place through the tail and find yourself in the reconstructed central blockhouse, which today serves as the gift shop and information center.

Inside, re-enactors hired by the local parks department work in period dress, tending the gardens and performing living history exhibitions. You can find them tending the garden (albeit with a modern garden hose) or making a fire in the hearth without the benefit of a Zippo.

The two-story complex inside the walls features the enlisted men's quarters, where soldiers slept dormitory style, as well as various guardhouses and the officers' quarters, which also contain the hospital room and garrison duty office.

Hoopes Melon Shed is a country farm stand selling produce and flowers just south of Muscatine, Iowa.

Over Memorial Day weekend, hundreds of bicyclists travel Highway 61 in Iowa. This group sails north toward Wapello.

A statue celebrates the area's Native American heritage in a riverfront park in Muscatine. It was presented to the city by the dubiously named "Improved Order of Red Men."

PRESENTED TO
THE CITY OF MUSCATINE
BY
MUSCUITINE TRIBE NO. 95
IMPROVED ORDER OF RED MEN
AND DEDICATED TO
THE MASCOUTIN INDIANS
1928

A memorial to the victims of September 11, 2001, is painted in the window of Herky's Bar, a favorite biker hangout, in Muscatine.

Lil' Lewie's Kitchen in Muscatine is a fine spot to grab an early breakfast along Highway 61.

The Catfish Bend Casino, viewed from Riverview Park in downtown Fort Madison, Iowa.

A Sunday Afternoon on the Island of Credit . . . with Apologies to Seurat

Credit Island juts out into the Mississippi on the southern edge of Davenport. A public golf course sits on the southern tip of the island, and the rest has been given over to basic shelters with grills and filthy bathrooms of the city park variety, the kind found in just about any town with at least one stoplight.

But with the Mississippi as a backdrop, it is something more: a lovable, if not lovely, place. A long road runs the length of the island, and along the right-hand side on your way south, a vaguely familiar scene captures the eye.

I pulled over to look, still unsure of why the damned things seemed so familiar. They were statues, along the bank, some lolling on their elbows, one tooting a bugle, others standing while looking out into the river. Then it dawned on me.

The scene I was looking at was a painting, or at least inspired by one. Given the fact that my deepest appreciation of art tends to revolve around the continuing adventures of *Mad Magazine*'s "Spy vs. Spy," I couldn't place the title or the artist, but odds were it was something French. After describing it to someone with a brain, I found out it was patterned after a painting by Georges Seurat, *A Sunday Afternoon on the Island of Grande Jatte*.

When the island flooded in 2001, some officials called to move the installation to Vander Veer Park, far up from the river. Originally crafted in wood, the sculptures had not weathered well even before the flood. But the sculptures remained. Now they are in the process of being coated in fiberglass to help protect them from the elements. Whether or not the sculptures are eventually moved, I suppose there are worse things than art for city fathers to argue about.

An art installation in Davenport's Credit Island Park recalls Georges Seurat's painting, Sunday Afternoon on the Island of Grande Jatte. The original statues were made of wood, but between the seasons and occasional flooding they did not weather well. They are slowly being re-covered in fiberglass.

A trumpeter looks out over the western shore of the Mississippi at Davenport, recalling the great jazz composer and Davenport product Bix Biederbecke. Every summer, the town of Davenport hosts a four-day Bix Beiderbecke Memorial Jazz Festival.

Davenport: Along Comes Mary

Mary, a former nurse who supplements her monthly disability payments by panhandling for change and cigarettes along Highway 61, posed for this photograph on Brady Street in downtown Davenport.

In Davenport, Iowa, Highway 61 follows the riverfront until Brady Street, where it runs up the hill and out of town, bypassing the other three Quad Cities. I lingered on the riverfront for a while, enjoying the sunny afternoon and watching the local fishermen cast wide nets into a shallow basin.

After stopping in to investigate a local brewpub, I walked back up the hill to Brady, where I had parked. I had just stowed my stuff when a soft voiced called behind me. "Excuse me. Would you like to share a cigarette?"

I turned around, doubly confused, wondering where this voice was coming from and how the person it belonged to could possibly know whether or not I smoked. Sitting back in the shadow of a storefront doorway was a woman of undetermined age who had obviously seen better times. She was covered in a filthy overcoat and a torn-up man's shirt, her hair having had no recent congress with a comb.

"Sure," I answered, patting my pockets in search of my smokes. They were jutting out of my back pocket, the second mystery now explained. I tossed her the pack.

She took a cigarette out and lit it, then leaned back and exhaled slowly with a satisfied smile.

A hydroelectric dam, operated by the Army Corps of Engineers, provides cheap electricity for the residents of the Quad Cities of Davenport and Bettendorf in Iowa, and Rock Island and Muscatine in Illinois.

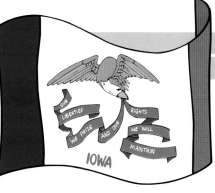

Her name was Mary. She gave me her last name as well, but I won't print it here, just in case she has changed her mind about it since.

"Coffee, pop, and cigarettes. They're my only bad habits," she said with a hoarse laugh.

Mary lived just across the river in Rock Island until she was 28. At the time, she was a registered nurse and gainfully employed. But one day she made a mistake that cost a patient his life.

"It was the right medication," she said looking down at her feet, "but I gave it to him the wrong way." Haunted by the incident, Mary left nursing and began drifting down and away from her former life. Saddled with a "no account" boyfriend, she was soon on the streets.

"The stress of it just got to me after that," she continued. "I couldn't go back and be a nurse anymore." When asked if there wasn't still some small part of her that might want to get back to the profession, she didn't speak but shook her head slowly from side to side, as she puffed her cigarette. "I come down here on Sunday afternoons to panhandle. I can't really walk much of a distance anymore, and this is the only place people come."

She is not homeless, but she is not far from it either. She had a hotel room paid up for another few days, then she didn't know what she would do. Perhaps go to Des Moines. She is legally blind, suffers from emphysema, and has been ignoring the clinic's advice to be tested for tuberculosis. Each month, she gets a $795

Bison roam a hillside on their ranch just outside of Blue Grass, Iowa, just outside Davenport. The animals are sold for breeding stock, skins, or meat.

disability check. When that runs low, the landlord runs a little store in one of the rooms where he sells cigarettes and other necessities on credit. The interest rate, payable when the checks come, is 50 percent.

"I don't know," she said, standing up and brushing her coat off. "I'd rather be doing anything than this . . . be out there, living out my heart's desires and everything. You know?" She held the pack of cigarettes up close to her face, counting, and looked up at me with a hooked eyebrow.

"Yeah, sure. Go ahead," I said.

She slid the half-pack into the pocket of her coat and started walking toward the river.

"Alright now. You send me one of those pictures now, alright? I'm at the Stricker 'til the seventh."

I tossed my stuff in the van as Mary walked into the first alley and sat down next to a garbage can. She lit a cigarette. Then she began yelling.

It was a garble mostly, what few words I could make out were usually cursing. She looked straight ahead for the most part, as if talking to someone a few feet in front of her. She was still going strong as I eased the van up the hill, past the light, and out of Davenport proper.

I sped north, thinking of her off and on for the 50 rolling miles through Grand Mound, Maquoketa, and Otter Creek before stopping on the south side of Dubuque for another pack of cigarettes.

The Front Street Brewery on the river's edge in Davenport, serves up pub food and freshly brewed beer, including Bucktown Stout, one of five different beers produced on site.

Give a man a fish, and he will eat for a day. Give him a net and a six pack, and you won't see him most weekends until October. Locals cast nets on the riverfront in Davenport, Iowa.

A painfully slow speed limit was imposed on motorists crossing the old Eagle Point Bridge heading into Wisconsin. LIBRARY OF CONGRESS

Dubuque, like just about every other Mississippi River town with a deficit and easily seduced politicians, has a casino—and the parade of suckers never seems to pass up any of them.

(61) Act III: Dickeyville to Pigeon River

More than 400 years old, the Witch Tree seems to grow from granite on Lake Superior's North Shore. Ojibwe who believed the tree had the power to calm the lake's waters, often left gifts there as insurance before taking trips on the lake. MINNESOTA OFFICE OF TOURISM

In the autumn, the southeast Minnesota bluff country is one of the upper Midwest's favorite destinations. The best road from which to view the fall colors? Highway 61, of course. MINNESOTA OFFICE OF TOURISM

There is a point on a roller-coaster when you reach the acme, when your stomach anticipates flying into your throat and you know that it is a long, fast, downhill run from here.

Cross the Mississippi again, this time into Wisconsin, while making jokes about cheese in the back of your mind. But then, standing at a gas pump as you fill up the beast, a guy walks up to you to ask you about the patch on your flight jacket. Before the tank is full, you both realize that you flew the same kind of spy plane, him in Vietnam, you in Beirut.

La Crosse is good for everything the Lord wants you to love, and it takes you over the river one last time into the Land of 10,000 Lakes, and nearer the end of the road.

To Red Wing and St. Paul. To Duluth and finally the glorious North Shore, where, though it is a thousand miles north of the worst parts of the South, they have murdered people because of the color of their skin.

The half of you that is Canadian longs for home.

From Iowa, Highway 61 continues north in Wisconsin before jumping across the Mississippi and into Minnesota from La Crosse. Glacial activity missed much of the area, which is thus known as the "driftless" region. The Eagle Point Bridge, which is, alas, no more, once carried 61 into Wisconsin. Library of Congress

The Patriot Priest

About 8 miles into America's Dairyland, you roll into the town of Dickeyville. Back in 1841, a surveyor from Pennsylvania set up a general store here and stayed for decades before moving to Kansas in 1872. But perhaps the town's most famous resident was a Slovenian priest who ministered to Dickeyville's German-Catholic population at Holy Ghost Church. In addition to his normal responsibilities at the church—conducting masses and baptizing and burying his parishioners—Father Mathias Wernerus constructed something that still draws up to 60,000 visitors a year: the grotto.

It is the sort of thing that, were you to try to build today, would never make it past the local planning commission. Working without blueprints, Wernerus began constructing his shrine to religion and patriotism out of just about anything he could find. He poured concrete over hand-built forms or in great slabs and, while it was still wet, would begin adorning it with chunks of colored glass, geodes from nearby fields, and even pieces of broken china brought in by parishioners.

Though referred to simply as "the grotto," Wernerus actually built several shrines over the years. There is the

Father Mathias Wernerus was a parish priest at the Holy Ghost Church in Dickeyville, Wisconsin, when he began building his famous grotto in 1920. Its main themes? Religion and patriotism.

original grotto, dedicated to the Blessed Virgin Mary, a shrine to Christ the King, the Sacred Heart of Jesus, and an altar in the parish cemetery. And, in dedication to patriotism, Wernerus installed shrines to Christopher Columbus, George Washington, and Abraham Lincoln.

The theme of patriotism was especially important to the priest. In the 1920s, anti-Catholic rhetoric was fairly common, and one of the central myths surrounding it was that Catholics put their allegiance to the Pope ahead of their loyalty to America. Even during the 1960 presidential election, John Kennedy was forced to dispel the same rumor.

After years of work, Wernerus finally completed his project in 1930. Almost 10,000 people visited it during its official dedication that September. Sadly, Wernerus passed away the following year at the age of 58.

Father Wernerus hoped that his life's work would become a place religious pilgrims could visit to affirm their faith. However, he was also afraid it would ultimately become commercialized; he wanted the grotto to remain a shrine to God and patriotism, not become an ice cream stand.

✦　✦　✦

Over the years the grotto remained a popular local attraction and a great source of parish pride. The years and the elements, however, started to take their toll. By 1995 many of the installations began to literally crumble, and the parish was caught in an odd bind. Since they had never charged admission or tried to make a profit on the grotto, they had not set aside any money for restoration. While they had a gift shop and a small box for donations out front, any moneys above and beyond the actual operating costs of the place were funneled directly into good works in their parish.

Then, what could fairly be called a miracle happened.

One day, a professional contractor, who was visiting his daughter at the University of Wisconsin in nearby Platteville, stopped by. The man had been a devout Christian his entire life and told the grotto manager he felt as if God had led him to the place. He volunteered a construction crew to lead the renovation if the parish would pay for the materials.

Father Wernerus used everything from poured concrete, to broken glass, to pieces of parishioners' broken plates in completing his life's work.

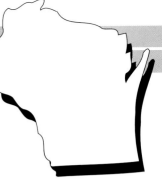

The entire parish volunteered their time, and like the initial construction, often brought in items to be used for decoration. The parish priest left a box outside the rectory for people to drop off items. Sometimes so many people showed up to help, the crew couldn't use them all and had to send them home.

The rehabilitation was completed in 1997. Every year since then, a group of volunteers has tended the grounds, planting flowers and keeping things neat. There is a running joke in the parish that some of the ladies are out there all day, just waiting for a weed to pop out so they can pluck it.

With the grotto once again structurally sound, there is talk among the parishioners of adding to the structure— perhaps a shrine to the right-to-life movement, or Our Lady of Fatima—but as of this writing, nothing has been decided for certain.

Father Mathias Wernerus worked without blueprints to build a shrine to patriotism and God, and in the process, he built a foundation for a community that has endured for seven decades after his death.

Just one of the many statues Father Wernerus installed on the grounds next to his German-American parish, Holy Ghost Church.

Christ the King, either holding a globe and scepter or having just returned from a game of softball, in the Dickeyville Grotto.

That Old-Time Religion

Samuel Hill (far right), a businessman from Beloit, Wisconsin, checked into the Central House Hotel in downtown Boscobel back in 1898. When John Nicholson (front) tried to check in later that day, the Central House was full up, but the clerk suggested he split lodgings with Hill, who had taken a room with two beds. Nicholson agreed, and later that night, the seeds were sown for an organization that still survives today. COURTESY THE GIDEONS INTERNATIONAL

There was no room at the inn . . . almost.

In 1865, after serving in the Civil War, a Prussian immigrant named Adam Bobel decided to build a saloon. He borrowed $5,000 and, with the help of a partner, erected a two-story building along Wisconsin Avenue, the main drag of Boscobel, Wisconsin. Construction was completed in six months, and after buying out his partner's interest, Bobel opened his saloon.

Like most public houses of the period, Bobel's saloon was a popular meeting spot for townsfolk, and the business thrived. Eight years later, he added a three-story hotel next door, the Central House. Located halfway between Galena, Illinois, and La Crosse, Wisconsin, the Central House soon became a popular stopover, renowned as one of the finest hotels in southwestern Wisconsin. In January 1881, a fire leveled the hotel, but Bobel rebuilt and reopened it in May of that year. He passed away four years later.

In the fall of 1898, a traveling salesman named John H. Nicholson from Janesville, Wisconsin, arrived in Boscobel and sought a room at the Central House. Unfortunately, the place was booked and the clerk

Today, the Central House Hotel has a thriving bar in the lobby.

suggested that Nicholson could share a room with another salesman who had a room with two beds. Nicholson agreed.

Nicholson settled in for the night with his new bunkmate, one Samuel Hill from Beloit, Wisconsin. After realizing they were both devout Christians, the two became fast friends. Nicholson told Hill that as a 12-year-old he had promised his dying mother that he would continue to read the Bible and pray daily, and was accustomed to doing so before he retired for the evening. The two men prayed together and discussed the need for some sort of Christian group that catered to the spiritual needs of travelers.

The next year, the two men met again in Beaver Dam, Wisconsin, and decided to hold a meeting for Christian travelers. They set the conference for July 1 at the YMCA in Janesville. Three people were present.

Hill, Nicholson, and their new friend, William Knights, met to discuss their goals. They decided to call

THE
CENTRAL HOUSE
HOTEL
HAS BEEN PLACED ON THE
NATIONAL REGISTER
OF HISTORIC PLACES
BY THE UNITED STATES
DEPARTMENT OF THE INTERIOR
BIRTHPLACE OF THE
GIDEON BIBLE
SEPTEMBER 14, 1898

their group the Gideons. Membership grew slowly and comprised almost entirely traveling salesmen. They wondered what the most effective way to minister to travelers would be, and finally struck upon the notion of putting a Bible that could be read by guests at the front desk of hotels. That notion ultimately expanded into putting a Bible in each room.

Within a decade, the organization grew considerably, and with funding from several church and ministerial groups, the Gideons began distributing Bibles nationwide. Today, the Gideons International distributes Bibles in 179 countries and in 80 different languages. They supply them, free for the asking, to hotels and motels, hospitals, prisons, and members of the armed forces.

Unlike many so-called evangelical organizations, the Gideons post their financial statements on their website for anyone to see. Instead of blaring their message from cable channels and UHF television stations with "prayer (read as 'donation') lines" plastered across the bottom of the screen, the Gideons' ministry is a soft-spoken one. If you open the bedside drawer in just about any motel or hotel in the country, you will find a Bible. You don't have to read it, of course, but for many folks, regardless of how religious they are, it is a small comfort to know it is there.

For that reason, the Gideons have never been lumped alongside the crooked televangelists or zealots that have embarrassed the Christian religion so often over the last 50 years. From their world headquarters in Nashville, Tennessee, they continue the good works started by Hill and Nicholson more than a century ago.

The Green Bay Packers are more than a mere football team in Wisconsin—for some fans, they're a religion. Here, the proprietor has posted a reminder in the window of his or her downtown Boscobel shop.

Some of the earliest Bibles distributed by the Gideons.
COURTESY THE GIDEONS INTERNATIONAL

Carl Henry Has the Coolest Job in the World

Heading north toward Winona, Minnesota, the JULIA BELLE SWAIN *departs for an afternoon on the river.* COURTESY JOAN COLLINS PUBLICITY

As a boy down in Hannibal, Missouri, young Sam Clemens and his friends watched the pilots who worked the river with admiration and respect. To be riverboat pilots "was our permanent ambition," he later wrote as Mark Twain. Clemens did indeed go on to become a pilot, and he used his on-the-job experiences as inspiration for his *Life on the Mississippi.*

Today, there are plenty of folks who drive boats up and down the Mississippi. Hundreds of tugboats and cruisers and gambling boats ply the waters between Minneapolis and New Orleans. Very few people, however, can say they are an authentic riverboat pilot.

It was late in the season, and a haze hung over the upper Mississippi River at La Crosse, Wisconsin. A light rain began to fall as Captain Carl Henry waved

High atop the JULIA BELLE SWAIN *sits the pilothouse. The boat's steering mechanism is controlled by a series of cables hooked to the wheel.* COURTESY JOAN COLLINS PUBLICITY

me up the narrow ladder to the pilothouse. He held up a finger, signaling me to wait a second as he leaned close in to hear the weather report. The wind started to pick up a bit, and while the boat he operated was indeed rare and historic, in bad weather, it steered like a hog on ice.

✦ ✦ ✦

Henry grew up in Mauston, Wisconsin, a small town just north of the Wisconsin Dells. There, while on summer break from college in 1980, he began his career on the water, driving "Ducks," the famous surplus World War II amphibious vehicles that take tourists through the Dells and onto the Wisconsin River.

"That's where I first got my Coast Guard license, was down in the Dells," he explained. "I don't think they require them now. I was working summers there, and when I came up here to go to college in La Crosse, I started working on some of the sightseeing boats

they had here, filling in as a relief pilot. Even after I graduated from college I kept working on boats like the *La Crosse Queen* and the *Island Girl*. That's when I started working on the Mississippi."

Once he graduated from the University of Wisconsin, Henry worked in advertising as an artist and graphic designer. But he always kept his Coast Guard license current and worked on boats part-time. The river kept calling, and after a while, Henry wanted to return.

He took three years off and worked on tugboats, pushing barges up and down the river, later returning to La Crosse to work the tourist boats there. When a chance opening for a pilot on the *Julia Belle Swain* came up, Henry pounced on it.

✦ ✦ ✦

A low rumbling came from the lower deck as the *Julia Belle* started making steam for her morning cruise. The weather was still dicey, but Captain Henry decided to

Captain Carl Henry guides the steamboat out of port and up the river on a breezy October morning.

take her out anyway. He reached up, grabbed the PA microphone, and greeted the passengers who had begun boarding.

"Good morning, and welcome aboard the *Julia Belle Swain*," he began in a gentle Wisconsin drawl. "The *Julia Belle Swain* is truly one of a kind, and one of a unique group of only five passenger steamboats in operation on the Mississippi River system.

"Her engines and related propulsion machinery were built in 1915. They are 87-year-old antique reciprocating steam engines that power the large, red paddlewheel in the back of the boat. There are no propellers or bow thrusters or other aids to propulsion. The *Julia Belle Swain* is considered to be the finest example of a stern-wheel steamboat that would have operated on this river more than 130 years ago . . . . Welcome aboard, and thanks for riding the *Julia Belle Swain*."

The passengers, all employees of a local manufacturer, milled about below and sipped coffee and Bloody Marys as the boat prepared to leave the dock. The boilers whooshed noisily and clouds of steam rose from the stern. To leave the dock, the *Julia Belle* didn't simply steam off, but drifted back slowly away from it, so there was good clearance before beginning her trip up stream.

As the huge paddle began turning, the calliope (pronounced *cal-EE-ope* on a riverboat) started playing, and many of the passengers walked to the back of the boat to watch steam shoot out the instrument's pipes.

Captain Henry pushed the *Julia Belle* north up the river, watching the darkening sky to the west.

"These boats just love nice hot, steamy summer weather," Henry said, leaning back on his chair and holding the massive steering wheel with one foot. The wheel itself is connected to the rudder below by two steel cables. Knowing how far the rudder is turned one way or the other is simple. There are two small marks painted near the end of the cable—if they are both lined up, the rudder is straight.

There is only one thing more beloved in the state of Wisconsin than its cheese, and perhaps even its Packers, and that is its beer. Here, a marcher in La Crosse's Oktoberfest parade shows his true colors. DENNIS CIESIELSKI

Oscar Mayer probably didn't know what a hit it had on its hands when it first produced a Weinermobile. Today it is as easily recognized as the Batmobile. DENNIS CIESIELSKI

"Once, a few years back, I was in a tornado," the captain continued. "It was on the *Island Girl*. It was a wall cloud that had tornado-speed winds. But it was a straight-line wind. It hit us and turned it into like a whiteout condition. It spun the boat around and around, and by the time we got out of it and could see where we were, we were about a mile down river."

Down in the main deck, passengers were settling into their breakfast as a local folk-rock duo, the Journeymen, strummed Ovation guitars. The wind started to pick up and a light rain began to fall. As if on cue, the Journeymen launched into the old Seals & Crofts tune, "Summer Breeze." In the pilothouse, Henry grabbed a microphone and called downstairs.

"Pilot to engineer."

"Yeah?" came the response.

"We're starting to get into a little bit of that wind now, so whatever pressure you can give me safely, OK?" Henry asked.

"You got it!"

As he told the passengers earlier, the *Julia Belle Swain* is a true stern-wheel paddleboat, while most others working the river are actually powered by diesel engines and propellers. The paddles on the back only turn for show, and don't actually move the boat—and that means she can't maneuver quickly.

"If you wanted to go from forward to reverse on this boat, it would take over a minute to do," Henry explained. "And if you really need to shift, that is the longest minute of your life."

Up ahead was a railroad bridge that needed to swing out of the way to let the *Julia Belle* pass. Henry radioed ahead to the bridge tender. For some reason, the wind suddenly died to nothing and the sun was shining brightly. Downstairs, the Journeymen kicked into the Beatles' "Here Comes the Sun." I joked that if I hear the opening chords to "The Wreck of the Edmund Fitzgerald" I'm grabbing a life vest. The bridge

Downtown La Crosse on a lazy Saturday afternoon.

eventually swung open and we steamed past, Henry waving to the bridge tender as we went.

"The best part of the job is getting to ride up and down the river and this just fantastic scenery," said Henry. "Plus, you get to meet and know a lot of people, and get to turn them on to the river and the history. You know, I grew up on a farm, so learning about all this stuff, from Mark Twain to the old riverboat days, that has become just as appealing to me as working on the boat."

As quickly as it appeared, the sun was gone, and the wind and rain came back with a vengeance. The *Julia Belle*'s pilothouse is an open one, and the rain began blowing inside. Henry closed the wooden door down to a crack and mopped the floor with a rag under his foot.

"I wouldn't have it any other way," he said, pointing out the open gap. "It's like you can really feel the river this way. I've driven other boats that had sealed windows, and once you get out at night, you can't see a thing. It's nothing but glare."

Henry, eyeing the sky again, radioed in for a weather update. It was not good. The storm was coming closer and growing stronger. There was one other small problem: a train was coming, which meant the

One of the inevitable effects of shutting down a town and serving beer for a week straight is a condition known as "beer goggles." DENNIS CIESIELSKI

swinging bridge behind us wouldn't be able to let us back through for a while. Henry conferred with his engineer, two decks down, and decided to head back.

He checked with the bridge tender, who told him the train was currently being held a few miles away, and that if he wanted to get back to port, he'd better do it quick. We steamed past the bridge as the wind howled outside.

Henry picked up his microphone and explained the situation to the passengers.

"Though we are not in any danger, your safety is always our first concern. It is not something we take lightly," he assured them

The passengers for the most part, took the news well. Since most of them were just sitting and chatting amongst themselves, it didn't seem to make much difference whether they were steaming upriver or sitting at the dock.

Henry guided the *Julia Belle* down below the dock and slowly brought her back upriver. A hand on the packer deck called out the distance to him over the intercom as he approached the dock.

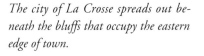

The city of La Crosse spreads out beneath the bluffs that occupy the eastern edge of town.

The Julia Belle Swain, *one of just a handful of true steamboats still working the Mississippi River, is shown docked at her home port of La Crosse.*

"Twenty feet . . . 15 feet . . . 10 . . . 6."

The great rumbling below dropped off, and the *Julia Belle Swain* drifted slowly to the dock. Deck hands jumped to shore and began tying her down to the massive cleats on the pier.

Carl Henry packed up his briefcase and climbed down the ladder out of the pilothouse. In a few days he would be steaming north to Minnesota on an overnight cruise. In the meantime, he'll be at home in Onalaska.

I stepped off the boat having realized two things: I had a sudden urge to reread Twain's *Life on the Mississippi,* and Carl Henry has the coolest job in the world.

The keyboard that controls the calliope is on the second deck of the Julia Belle Swain.

It takes the Julia Belle Swain *a few minutes to build up enough steam to head up the river. Once her boilers are going full, the calliope can begin playing through these pipes.*

An all-American town. Downtown Winona, Minnesota, one of the Julia Belle Swain's *ports of call, comes complete with a hill-top flag.*

Over the River and through the Woods

I stayed in La Crosse an extra day, spending the night with some dear friends who never fail to stuff me full of excellent vegetarian food, good wine, and stimulating conversation. When those run out, the guitars and the scotch bottle inevitably come out. As someone whose adolescent soundtrack was the Neil Young discography, I was amused and confused the following morning to realize that we had spent a good chunk of the night before working out a version of an old song called "Calcutta" by Lawrence Welk. There is a difference between aging and aging gracefully. Apparently, I have yet to figure it out.

I'm addicted to many things, the least dangerous of which is a fix of news in the morning. On the home front, it is the *Chicago Tribune*. On the road, it is usually that spot on the AM dial that every community seems to have reserved for some station offering "all news, all the time."

I fired up the van and pounded the radio buttons until a news station popped up. The dogs of war were barking loudly. We already had troops in Afghanistan, and from what the reports were saying, it seemed the folks in Washington, D.C., were gearing up for another little spot of fun in Iraq.

With that in mind, I couldn't help but notice the irony as I left La Crosse, Wisconsin and went over the Mississippi into La Crescent, Minnesota. The Cross and the Crescent . . . Wisconsin and Minnesota . . . Christianity and Islam, all with a wide and dangerously impassible gulf between them.

There was little else in the news that morning, and the story and feeling of impending war followed me along Highway 61 as I headed north for the Twin Cities, where I planned to stop for the night. The highway follows the river for the most part, sometimes within view, sometimes a mile or so away. Little towns like

On Highway 61 just south of La Crosse, Wisconsin, a brief beam of sunshine illuminates the terraced farmland on an otherwise rainy afternoon.

The real "King of Beers?" According to folk tale, Gambrinus, the King of Flanders, was also the patron saint of beer. This statue depicting Gambrinus stands outside the former Heileman brewery in La Crosse.

The "World's Largest Six Pack" is located on Highway 61 in La Crosse. Once owned by the Heileman Brewing Company, the towers at one time were painted with the Old Style can design seen here. If you travel there today, you'll find six tall, gray cylinders. ERIC DREGNI. A sign next to the World's Largest Six Pack" enumerates the amount of beer typically held therein. A six pack a day for 3,351 years? No wonder residents call Wisconsin "God's Country."

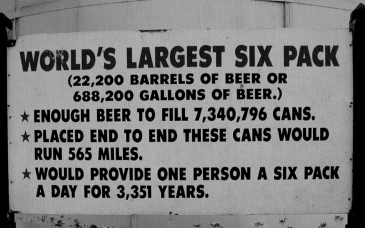

WORLD'S LARGEST SIX PACK
(22,200 BARRELS OF BEER OR 688,200 GALLONS OF BEER.)
★ ENOUGH BEER TO FILL 7,340,796 CANS.
★ PLACED END TO END THESE CANS WOULD RUN 565 MILES.
★ WOULD PROVIDE ONE PERSON A SIX PACK A DAY FOR 3,351 YEARS.

Highway 61 jumps across the Mississippi River at La Crosse and enters Minnesota. The view on the right is looking north up the Mississippi from the bridge.

Goodview, Weaver, and Read's Landing break up the monotony along the way. I pulled into Lake City a few hours after leaving La Crosse and paused to walk along the river there, watching pleasure craft return from a day on the river and barges slowly ply their way south.

When I left an hour or so later, the radio was predicting something else—snow. It was getting late in the season, and while I was heading into Minnesota during the absolute perfect time for viewing the fall colors, I was also one high-pressure system away from having it all covered in snow before I could point a camera at it. I had to make good time if I was going to get to Canada before the snow started to fly.

Bush. Saddam. "Weapons of Mass Destruction." If I had any brains I would have just shut the goddamned radio off, but I returned to it again and again, listening for updates, the way a tongue returns to torture itself against a chipped tooth.

Back in the city, when I grow disgusted with myself, or with the world in general, there is a little patch of woods down on the Des Plaines River that I call my own. I find solace there among the trees and the herd of deer that live under the roaring of jets from O'Hare Airport. Although I was now racing north against the weather, something told me that what I needed most at this particular moment was not another generic motel room, an evening of delivery pizza, and CNN. About the same time I came to that realization, I saw the sign pointing to Frontenac State Park.

I turned off the highway and headed for the park. Just before the entrance, I saw a huge pile of firewood in the yard of a farmhouse. I pulled up next to the pile and saw a note stuck a to small box: "Five bucks a wheelbarrow load. Help yourself. Leave the money in the box." I did.

I stopped and registered with the park office and wound my way back into the hilltops looking for a secluded spot. I quickly set up camp, readied the fire, and rummaged around in the cooler for something to cook for dinner.

The weather had turned cloudy by late afternoon, and since I was under a large canopy of trees, it was already near dark. I lit the fire, banking it well to counter the dropping temperature. After dinner, I made a pot of

The town of La Crescent is the first stop in Minnesota along Highway 61.

coffee and enjoyed the smell of it brewing. I poured myself a cup, leaving room for a healthy dollop of whiskey, and walked over to the van to turn on the radio. I wasn't much in the mood for any more news, so I switched to FM and headed for the NPR end of the dial, hoping to find some jazz or blues.

When I finally got a signal, I was pleased to hear some kind of hillbilly swing music. I grabbed my coffee and sat down near the fire, wrapping myself in a blanket. When the music ended, there was a quick round of applause, then a soothing voice said, "It's been a quiet week in Lake Wobegon."

Lake Pepin licks the shoreline as the sun begins to set over Lake City.

The 61 Motel is located alongside, you guessed it, Highway 61 in Frontenac.

The "lake" in Lake City, Minnesota, is Lake Pepin, which is actually a wide spot in the Mississippi River and a favorite among recreational boaters.

La Crosse has Gambrinus; Frontenac, Minnesota, has St. Hubert. The lodge shown here prior to World War II was founded in 1855 by General Israel Garrard and named after the patron saint of hunters. Today, St. Hubert's is a fully appointed and award-winning bed and breakfast. LIBRARY OF CONGRESS

Great River Bluffs State Park not only overlooks Highway 61 and the Mississippi River Valley between La Crosse and Winona; come autumn, it provides some spectacular scenery. MINNESOTA OFFICE OF TOURISM

In addition to its eponymously named brand of work boots, Red Wing is also well-known for its pottery. In 1878, Red Wing Stoneware Company was founded along what would become Highway 61 just north of town. Ever since, collectors have clamored for Red Wing jugs and bowls sporting everything from the Hamm's bear to the "sponge panel" design on this specimen.
JOHN KOHARSKI

A field of sumac appears no worse for the wear after an early frost at Frontenac State Park in southeastern Minnesota.

In 1891, the state of Minnesota opened the State Training School for Boys and Girls to "counteract the results of idleness and evil companionship by moral and intellectual instruction." That mission statement would prove ironical—over the years tales of inmate abuse at the hands of some reformatory guards became the stuff of legend and were immortalized by Bob Dylan in his song "Walls of Red Wing." Students are shown here in the school's manual training shop, circa 1920. MINNESOTA STATE HISTORICAL SOCIETY, NEG. 15701

The old train depot at Red Wing, a Minnesota river town renowned for the brand of boots that bears its name.

"Oh, the age of the inmates
I remember quite freely:
No younger than twelve,
No older 'n seventeen . . .
Inside the walls,
The walls of Red Wing."

—*Bob Dylan, "Walls of Red Wing"*

Garrison Keillor: The Best Bassoon Player in Anoka

William Faulkner had Mississippi, Stephen King has Maine, and Garrison Keillor has Minnesota. Each week on his radio variety program, *A Prairie Home Companion,* he takes listeners to a little place he calls home: Lake Wobegon, Minnesota.

The two-hour broadcast mixes live music, sketch comedy, and fake ads into a gentle spoof of Minnesota and Minnesotans. It's a comforting look back at the innocence of the American small town. It's *The Lawrence Welk Show* for people who smoked pot in their younger days. It is also quite good, better than most people realize.

There is no Lake Wobegon, of course. But for Keillor's audience, his fictional hometown has become as dear to them as their own. If you grew up in the Midwest, you know these characters. In fact, you are one.

◆　◆　◆

Keillor was born in 1942 in Anoka, just north of Minneapolis. After receiving a B.A. in English from the University of Minnesota in 1966, he got on a bus heading to New York City, ready to conquer the literary world. He landed in a boarding house on West 19th Street and got job interviews with *Sports Illustrated, The Atlantic,* and *The New Yorker,* but none of them hired him. A month or so later, he returned to Minnesota.

He kept writing short stories and submitting them

Garrison Keillor, author and host of the popular A Prairie Home Companion *radio program is a St. Paul fixture.* Jason Bell

A live performance of A Prairie Home Companion *at the Fitzgerald Theater in downtown St. Paul. From left to right are sound-effects man Tom Keith, actors Tim Russell and Sue Scott, and Keillor.* Cheryl Walsh Bellville

to magazines in New York. Eventually his persistence paid off when in 1969 *The New Yorker* published one of his stories. That same year, he began working for Minnesota Public Radio, hosting a morning program that, while called *A Prairie Home Companion,* had little in common with the current show, save having Keillor as a host.

In the early 1970s, while working on an assignment about the Grand Ole Opry for *The New Yorker*, he was struck with an idea. He wanted to create something similar—a radio show with musical guests. On July 6,

1974, Keillor stepped on stage in the auditorium at Macalester College in St. Paul for the first live broadcast of the new *A Prairie Home Companion.* There were 12 people in the audience.

These days, the show is broadcast on more than 500 radio stations and is carried by Armed Forces Radio in Europe and Asia. Most stations carry it live, and between that and the overseas rebroadcasts, its audience numbers roughly three million.

Visitors inside the St. Paul City Hall and Ramsey County Courthouse are greeted by Vision of Peace, *a 36-foot, 60-ton Mexican onyx statue carved by the Swedish sculptor Carl Milles. The work was unveiled in 1936 and was inspired by Native American ceremonies.* Eric Dregni

Like the old slave quarters pictured in Chapter 2, the City Hall and County Courthouse in St. Paul was also photographed for the Historic American Building Survey. Many consider the building to be one of the most stunning examples of Depression-era public architecture. Library of Congress

The centerpiece of every broadcast is Keillor's monologue, "The News from Lake Wobegon." It runs 10 to 15 minutes and is delivered without a visible script. It is pure genius. In his trademark tuxedo and red socks, Keillor, an admittedly shy person, weaves the stories of Lake Wobegon's residents deftly and quietly, sometimes almost whispering the news like a rumor. It is a dispatch from an ordered world.

The people of Lake Wobegon shop at Ralph's Pretty Good Grocery. They often dine at the Chatterbox Café. And when they are in need of a drink, they take it at the Sidetrack Tap. They have an unhealthy preoccupation with the quality of their neighbors' gardens and often worry about Pastor Inkvist's daydreaming and Alma Lindbergh. One poor resident had made the mistake of answering to the nickname "Booger" years ago and has been saddled with it ever since. And although there are whispers about her techniques, it is common knowledge that Irene Bunsen's tomatoes possess a kind of magic.

Years ago, when I was living on Cape Cod, I tuned in religiously to WGBH to hear the news. I began to realize that, as comforting as Keillor's stories were, they also described the very things about a small town that I fled years before. The notion that everyone in town knew you and why you got suspended from school in second grade—that your life was an open book and

A line of barges anchored on the upper Mississippi in St. Paul await a trip down river.

Cartoonist Charles Schulz was another of St. Paul's famous natives. Each year, he is honored throughout the city with larger-than-life statues of his beloved PEANUTS characters, no two of which are decorated alike. Here, Lucy Van Pelt, amateur psychotherapist and nemesis of PEANUTS' main character, good ol' Charlie Brown, offers up some pharmaceuticals on a plaza in downtown St. Paul.

there were an inordinate number of book critics in the area. While there is a sense of comfort in small-town life, there is a sense of freedom in a big city where no one knows you.

Perhaps Keillor realized this as well.

In June 1987 after 13 years, he ended the show and moved to New York City. Two years later, he founded The American Radio Company and began broadcasting from the Brooklyn Academy of Music. In time, the new program was picked up by more than 200 stations. But it seems Minnesota was his muse, and in 1992, he announced he was moving the program back to his home state. A year later, he dropped The American Radio Company name and broadcast it again as *A Prairie Home Companion*. In 1994, he was inducted into the Radio Hall of Fame in Chicago.

And so it goes.

Today, *A Prairie Home Companion* is something of a cottage industry, selling coffee mugs, T-shirts, and ball caps online and through their catalog business. They have a retail outlet in the Mall of America in Bloomington, Minnesota.

Keillor takes the show on the road once in a while, but more often than not it is broadcast live from the Fitzgerald Theater in downtown St. Paul. He continues to mine the depths—and the shallows—of Lake

A sign outside the Fitzgerald Theater announces it as the home to performances of A Prairie Home Companion.

The only operational dining car in Minnesota, Mickey's has been in business 24/7 since 1937, when the structure was moved to the corner of 9th and St. Peter Streets on a flatbed truck from its manufacturer in New Jersey. The streamlined Art Deco classic is just around the corner from the Fitzgerald Theater, where broadcasts of Garrison Keillor's A Prairie Home Companion *originate.* Eric Dregni

Wobegon in his monologues and novels. He produces the "Writer's Almanac" segment for Minnesota Public Radio, and for a spell, he was an advice columnist for the online magazine Salon.com.

Today, the bard of the Norwegian Bachelor Farmers actually lives across the Mississippi in River Falls, Wisconsin. He also maintains a home in New York City. Although he has always been a writer, he will probably go down in history as the host of *A Prairie Home Companion* and the man who explained to the rest of America the mystery that is *lutefisk*.

Yet from his early days in an $80-a-month farm-house to the icon he has become, Keillor has kept his Wobegonian humility.

"Writing is a sacred calling," he told *The Atlantic Monthly* in a 1997 interview. "So are gardening, dentistry, and plumbing."

The brownstone rowhouses at 593 and 599 Summit Avenue in St. Paul are better known as the "Fitzgerald House" and the place where one of the city's most famous sons, the great novelist F. Scott Fitzgerald (namesake of the Fitzgerald Theater), wrote his first novel, THIS SIDE OF PARADISE. *Fitzgerald described the brownstone as "a house below the average on a street above the average."* LIBRARY OF CONGRESS

When F. Scott Fitzgerald learned in 1919 that a publisher back in New York had purchased his first novel, THIS SIDE OF PARADISE, *he ran up and down St. Paul's Summit Avenue, stopping motorists to tell them the news.* MINNESOTA STATE HISTORICAL SOCIETY, NEG. 75625

El Dorado Conquistador Musuem:
Where Conquest is Kitsch
by Eric Dregni

Spurred by the Broadway smash *Man of La Mancha* in the late 1960s and early 1970s, entrepreneurs across America began cashing in on the craze, much to the delight of not-so-refined consumers across the nation.

Cervantes had hit prime time, and all things Spanish were the rage. The quixotic search for adventure amidst suburban sprawl was a mere redecoration away, as greedy connoisseurs snatched black velvet matadors and foam conquistadors off store shelves. The gruesome deeds of Cortez were forgotten and impaled, bleeding bulls were immortalized in oil and velvet. Today, those smells of danger that could once be savored in the safety of your sitting room are painstakingly preserved in one St. Paul museum.

With more than 50 conquistador masterpieces in various mediums ranging from pressed plastic to black velvet and hardened foam, The El Dorado Conquistador Museum, housed in a basement at the William Mitchell College of Law, boasts the largest collection of conquistador kitsch in the world.

At El Dorado, located a stone's throw from F. Scott Fitzgerald's boyhood home on posh Summit Avenue, every attempt is made to re-create the unsanitary conditions of both a 1970s rec room and the Middle Ages when the Black Plague ran rampant. The carpet has been carefully stained, comfortable plush lounge chairs are seldom vacuumed, and moldy Cheetos have been studiously placed beneath the cushions. In an attempt at state-of-the-art, interactive, multisensory displays, a toilet's flushing can be heard near the Galleon Gallery, simulating the battering waves upon the bow of a Spanish ship in search of plunder.

After all, this is El Dorado, the mythical city of gold. This is paradise, found at last.

Housed in a basement at the William Mitchell College of Law in St. Paul, the El Dorado Conquistador Museum boasts the largest collection of conquistador kitsch in the world. As of early 2004, there was speculation the collection would move to a nightclub in "Dinkytown," Robert Zimmerman's old stomping grounds near the University of Minnesota. Mark Vesley and the Conquistador Museum Archive

Bob Dylan Will Die for Your Sins: The Conscience of America Was Born in Duluth

On September 29, 1961, Nikita Kruschev, on vacation at the Black Sea, dashed off a letter to President John F. Kennedy concerning Germany. In Paris, Rudolf Nureyev slipped away from his KGB handlers and defected to French authorities. And in New York, a short music review by Robert Shelton ran in the *New York Times*.

"A bright new face in folk music is appearing at Gerde's Folk City," Shelton began. "Although only 20 years old, Bob Dylan is one of the most distinctive stylists to play the Manhattan cabaret in months. Resembling a cross between a choirboy and a beatnik, Mr. Dylan has a cherubic look and a mop of tousled hair he partly covers with a Huck Finn black corduroy hat. His clothes may need a bit of tailoring, but when he works his guitar, harmonica, or piano and composes songs faster that he can remember them, there is no doubt he is bursting at the seams with talent."

Shelton continued his praise for several more paragraphs, weighing the performer's vocal ability, his dramatic stage presence, and his choice of material. He finally summed it all up with the closing line, "It matters less where he has been than where he is going, and that seems to be straight up."

Bob Dylan was born.

Robert Allen Zimmerman, on the other hand, was born in Duluth, Minnesota, on May 24, 1941. His family moved to Hibbing, 76 miles to the north, in 1947. He had an unremarkable childhood by all accounts. Zimmerman began writing poetry at age 10 and, by his early teens, had taught himself how to play guitar and piano.

Like most teenagers in the late 1950s, he was entranced by the new sounds of rock n' roll and, while in high school, performed in such bands as the Golden Chords and Elston Gunn and his Rock Boppers. He left the iron-mining town of Hibbing in 1959 to attend the University of Minnesota—some 200 miles south on Highway 61—but by then was so devoted to music that he only attended classes sporadically.

For better or worse, Bob Dylan's toughest competition has always been his past. He continues to write, record, and tour, but today's Dylan is not the force that he was when he released HIGHWAY 61 REVISITED. *That's not a knock against Dylan—music is simply no longer the force it once was.* COLUMBIA RECORDS

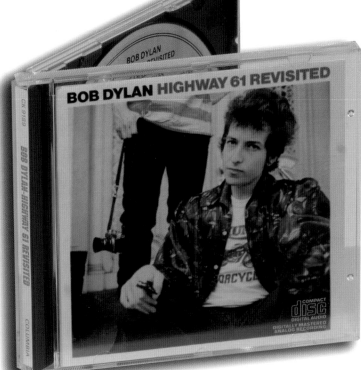

Bob Dylan's famous album, with a cover photograph by Daniel Kramer, inspired thousands of songwriters and music fans alike. COLUMBIA RECORDS

Instead, he began studying the roots of rock n' roll music, the old country and blues and folk records that preceded the current day's hits. He also began writing his own music and performing it at the Ten O'Clock Scholar in Minneapolis and the Purple Onion Pizza Parlor in St. Paul. Somewhere along the line, Robert Zimmerman became Bob Dylan.

Ground zero for the burgeoning folk music scene in those days, however, was Greenwich Village in New York City, and after dropping out of college in 1961, that's where Dylan went. By all reports, he had two main goals in mind: to become part of the developing folk scene and to meet an aging singer who was slowly dying in a New Jersey hospital—Woody Guthrie.

Guthrie was an important influence on Dylan, who visited Guthrie often, sometimes performing the ailing singer's songs for him as he lay in bed. In some ways, it seemed the early Dylan was channeling Guthrie, from his talking blues to his workingman ethos with rolled up sleeves.

Dylan was signed to Columbia Records by legendary producer John Hammond and began recording his self-titled first album, a mix of original songs and country and blues chestnuts. It was an immediate hit, and soon Dylan was being whispered about as "the new Woody Guthrie."

His second album, *The Freewheelin' Bob Dylan,* established him as an artist in his own right. That record not only contained songs, it contained the anthems "Hard Rain's A-Gonna Fall" and "Blowin' in the Wind."

There were two basic things that set Dylan apart from the others early in his career. Although he banged a guitar as well as anyone on the folk music scene, his

This bird's-eye view of downtown Duluth was taken in the 1970s. LIBRARY OF CONGRESS

An observation point south of town provides a wonderful view of the polluted St. Louis Bay, where the St. Louis River enters Lake Superior in West Duluth.

A Mobil gas station in Duluth's Canal Park shopping district, once the city's red-light waterfront, is decked out with retro signage.

and he showed every kid in America with a cheap guitar and three chords under his belt that they could do it too, if they really wanted.

With each album that followed, Dylan grew not only as a writer and musician, but also as a force in American music. Other bands covered his songs, turning them into top 40 hits. He began a romance with folksinger Joan Baez, and they became counterculture royalty in the process.

But Dylan was growing out of the folk music scene. When he hit the stage at the Newport Folk Festival in 1965, slinging a Stratocaster and with the Paul Butterfield Blues Band backing him, purists were horrified. He was vilified by folkies who thought that by strapping on an electric guitar he had somehow sold out.

Also in 1965, Dylan released an album called *Highway 61 Revisited*, from which the title of this book is lovingly borrowed. Which Highway 61 was he talking about: the one that ran through his boyhood home of Duluth or the one that traversed the Mississippi Delta? It was as good as anything he had done to date.

voice was what could be diplomatically called a "unique instrument." In an age where pop music leaned to harmonizing quartets and solo crooners, it was almost unthinkable that a fellow who sang like that could get a gig, much less a record contract.

Secondly, his songs were topical and, above all, angry. Like Guthrie decades before, Dylan wrote about little people and their plights, and spit these realities into the face of an uncaring, or unaware, American public. He wrote them himself, he sang them himself,

Also in Canal Park, Duluth's famous lift bridge raises to allow pleasure craft and freighters alike to pass from Lake Superior proper to ore docks, grain elevators, and marinas located on the other side of Park Point.

Dylan Does Duluth
by Tony Dierckins

Bob Dylan came into this world at Duluth's St. Mary's Hospital as Robert Zimmerman. He lived with his parents, Abe (a supervisor for Standard Oil Company) and Beatrice, on the second floor of a duplex and attended Nettleton School. When young Bob was six years old his family moved north to Hibbing, his mother's hometown.

On January 31, 1959, high school senior Zimmerman hitched a ride to Duluth to see Buddy Holly and the Crickets, J. P. "The Big Bopper" Richardson, Ritchie Valens, and Dion & the Belmonts play at the National Guard Armory on London Road. He had a third-row seat. Two nights later, Holly, the Big Bopper, and Valens gave their final show in Clear Lake, Iowa, and died in a plane crash. In his 1998 Grammy Award acceptance speech, Dylan recalled the concert and claimed to have made eye contact with Holly. The Armory, once on the Preservation Alliance of Minnesota's list of Ten Most Endangered Historic Properties, may be renovated by a local arts group.

Dylan has played in Duluth twice. His first appearance was at the Duluth Entertainment and Convention Center Arena in the fall of 1998, during which he did not acknowledge his hometown in words. During his second appearance, outdoors on July 3, 1999, at Bayfront Park, he pointed up toward his childhood home on the Hillside and joked about an old girlfriend.

Tony Dierckins is a Duluth-based publisher and the author, along with Kerry Elliott, of True North: Alternate and Off-Beat Destinations in and Around Duluth Superior and Shores of Lake Superior.

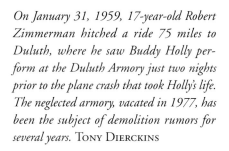

On January 31, 1959, 17-year-old Robert Zimmerman hitched a ride 75 miles to Duluth, where he saw Buddy Holly perform at the Duluth Armory just two nights prior to the plane crash that took Holly's life. The neglected armory, vacated in 1977, has been the subject of demolition rumors for several years. TONY DIERCKINS

Bob Dylan was born Robert Zimmerman upstairs in this duplex at 519 North Third Avenue in Duluth, and spent the first six years of his life there. The house made headlines in June 2001 when it was sold on the Internet auction site eBay for $94,600. TONY DIERCKINS

In 2000, Spinout Records released DULUTH DOES DYLAN, *on which 15 Duluth acts covered songs written by that town's favorite native son. Adorned with cover art by local cartoonist Chris Monroe, the resulting tribute platter represented the entire range of the port city's burgeoning music scene, from slo-core indie darlings Low to the boozy, barroom swagger of Giljunko.* COURTESY SPINOUT RECORDS

The next year, on July 29, Dylan was involved in a near-fatal motorcycle accident that broke his neck. Miraculously, he recovered and holed up in Woodstock, New York. Over the next few years, he released *John Wesley Harding* and *Nashville Skyline*, but did not perform live. By 1970, when *Self Portrait* was released, Dylan, who once had reverent fans, now had skeptics. *Rolling Stone* magazine, which had sung his praises for years, actually asked, "What is this shit?"

In August 1971, Dylan appeared on stage for the first time since his accident as part of George Harrison's Concert for Bangladesh. Throughout the rest of the 1970s he continued recording, producing both hits and misses. By the end of the decade, he had left fans scratching their heads again, becoming first a born-again Christian then, two albums later, embracing conservative Judaism. Dylan was still growing and changing. Some fans stayed on for the ride, others heard The Clash's *London Calling* and embraced the punk movement.

By the mid-1980s, Dylan had sublimated his solo career and joined a band. He toured with Tom Petty and the Grateful Dead. In 1988, he formed the Traveling Wilburys with Petty, George Harrison, Roy Orbison, and Jeff Lynne.

For better or worse, Bob Dylan's worst competition has always been his past. He continues to write, record, and tour, but today's Dylan is not the force that he was in 1965. That's not a knock against him—music is simply no longer the force it once was. Themes of social injustice just don't sell records anymore. Today's rightful heirs to Dylan the poet and speaker of truth are rappers, but given that most hip-hop seems more concerned with the thickness of wallets and sexual prowess, they come off as petty and self-absorbed. Anger does not necessarily equal relevance.

In the end, perhaps the truest measure of Dylan's importance to American music and culture is this: for 40 years, music critics trying to find a phrase to describe an up-and-coming singer/songwriter have typically described him as "the next Bob Dylan."

And in all those years, they've never been right.

A small coast guard craft returns to port after an afternoon patrolling Lake Superior.

The SS WILLIAM A. IRVIN, *a former U.S. Steel freighter, is permanently docked on the Duluth waterfront and open for daily tours.* ERIC DREGNI

The Infamous Duluth Lynchings
by Tony Dierckins

Like any city, Duluth has had some ugly moments in its past, but none more horrible than June 15, 1920. The John Robinson Show Circus was in town the previous day for two performances in West Duluth. Later that night, 18-year-old Duluthian James Sullivan claimed that a black man from the circus held a pistol to his head and forced him to watch five other black circus workers rape Irene Tusken, 19, also from Duluth. It was a lie. A doctor who examined Tusken found no signs of sexual assault, yet he did not report his findings to authorities. Police rounded up a group of black circus workers and eventually held several of them, including Elmer Jackson, Elias Clayton, and material witness Isaac McGhie, all between 19 and 21 years old.

Though not reported in the newspapers, news of the alleged rape spread through West Duluth, where outraged businessman Louis Dondino began rounding up a mob, causing a chain reaction throughout the community. By 8:40 P.M. a riotous group of an estimated 10,000 people stormed the downtown jail on Superior Street. By 9:30 they had broken through. After beating and harassing the prisoners, the mob took Jackson and Clayton—and later, McGhie—a block away to the corner of First Street and Second Avenue East. Some tried to stop the mob, including Reverend W. J. Powers, who climbed a light pole to address the crowd. The mob pulled him down and used the same light pole and some rope to kill Jackson, Clayton, and McGhie. The killers then posed for photographs next to their victims before a militia arrived and dispersed the crowd. Later, the photos were sold as postcards and eventually inspired Bob Dylan to include the line "They're selling postcards of the hanging" in his 1965 song "Desolation Row." The only punishments given to members of the lynch mob were convictions of rioting.

In the 1940s, a St. Louis County Historical Society employee discarded records of the incident, deeming it too unseemly for study by students at the Duluth Normal School (now the University of Minnesota at Duluth). In 2003, the Clayton Jackson McGhie Memorial Committee established a memorial to the lynching victims on the very street corner where they were killed.

Tony Dierckins is a Duluth-based publisher and the author, along with Kerry Elliott, of True North: Alternate and Off-Beat Destinations in and Around Duluth Superior and Shores of Lake Superior.

In 2003 a memorial to Jackson, Clayton, and McGhie was unveiled at the corner of First Street and Second Avenue East in Duluth, the site of the hanging. Duluth Convention and Visitors Bureau

The scene at the downtown Duluth jail on June 16, 1920, the day after a mob broke in and dragged out Elmer Jackson, Elias Clayton, and Isaac McGhie, circus workers who were falsely accused of raping a local woman. Minnesota State Historical Society, Neg. 13949

The North Shore

Located in Two Harbors is Pierre the Voyageur, a 20-foot statue constructed of telephone poles and stucco. Located next to the Voyageur Motel, Pierre used to have movable eyes that followed travelers as they passed by on Highway 61. ERIC DREGNI

Just outside the northern edge of Duluth, there is a little building—not much more than a shack, really—that serves as the official gateway to Lake Superior's North Shore. There, volunteers hand out maps, give advice, and watch the world's largest freshwater lake lap up against the shore. For all of those volunteers' good intentions, however, it in no way prepares you for what lies ahead.

I have traveled all over the world in the last 25 years, from quaint villages in northern England, to bustling cities in Pinochet's Chile. I've sipped espresso on the Taromina waterfront, watched the sun rise over the Alps, and smoked hash with British ex-patriots (and fugitives) in the Greek Islands. But simply put, I have never seen anything like this.

In its last stretch toward the Canadian border, Highway 61 clings to the shoreline of Lake Superior. What once were remote fishing villages are now remote tourist destinations, and between them, rivers crash out of black stone hillsides into the lake below. Hills rise to the west, and the gray-blue of Superior stretches to the east as far as the eye can see.

It is about 160 miles from Duluth to the Canadian border, and after this long on the road, you stop thinking about miles and start calculating distance in hours (i.e., 160 miles equals two-and-a-half to three hours). But that doesn't count time to stop and gawk, to walk the shoreline, or to climb a rocky hillside for a better view. If there is anything maddening about the process, it is that once you have stopped, taken in the pristine scene, and gotten back in the car, 5 miles later there is another river, another vista, better than the one before. Yes, you can make it to Canada in a few hours, but you won't want to. You'll soon wish you could trade your Ford for a horse or a sturdy pair of hiking boots.

✦　　✦　　✦

The massive ore docks at Two Harbors, shown here in 1909, have sent countless tons of iron ore and taconite off to steel mills in the East. LIBRARY OF CONGRESS

It was the first week of October and high season for fall colors. The snow they had been predicting when I was still south of Duluth had stayed in Canada, but a new front was moving in. I had two days, maybe three, before it hit the fan.

I gazed at the cedar-clapped cottages that dotted the shoreline and felt a mix of envy and pity. I envied the owners for the obvious value of their property and the fact they lived so near the water, but in the same respect felt sorry for them. Was it possible they had become immune to the beauty outside their windows? Did they even see it anymore? Was the lake a source of wonder and awe, or merely a brute force that pummeled them during bad weather?

A pair of fishermen compare bait as the sun rises over Lake Superior just north of Duluth.

The docks still operate today and are a popular tourist attraction.

✦　✦　✦

The villages that populate the North Shore are much the same. Mostly descended from fishing villages, they hope for some tourist trade. Their names invariably end in "River" or "Bay." It's about 30 miles to Two Harbors, the site of famous ore docks. They are a mind-boggling sight. Jutting out into the lake, their rusting frames resemble chunks of the Death Star fallen from space.

Everywhere you look, especially in the autumn, you see postcard views. There is one sight in particular that has become almost synonymous with the beauty of Minnesota's North Shore. It has been reproduced in a thousand postcards and calendars and in bits of promotional materials from local chambers of commerce—it sits atop Split Rock.

Betty's Pies, a favorite stop for generations of North Shore travelers, began decades ago as a fish shack.

Favorite haunts among fishermen are the numerous trout and salmon streams entering the North Shore of Lake Superior between Duluth and the Canadian border. Here, an old concrete arch bridge spans a creek emptying into Lake Superior, north of Duluth.

BAKED
Slice- $2.95 Whole- $15.00
STRAWBERRY PEACH CRUNCH
BUMBLEBERRY
BLACKBERRY PEACH

PUMPKIN
PECAN
PEACH
SUGAR FREE BUMBLEBERRY
BLUEBERRY
APPLE RASPBERRY CRUNCH
BLUEBERRY PEACH CRUNCH
APPLE
STRAWBERRY RHUBARB
SPICY APPLE CRUNCH

CREAM
Slice- $2.95 Whole- $15.00
5 LAYER BUTTERSCOTCH
5 LAYER CHOCOLATE
STRAWBERRY BANANA CREAM
COCONUT
BANANA CREAM
SOUR CREAM RAISIN
LEMON ANGEL
FRENCH APPLE CREAM
CHOCOLATE BANANA CREAM
FRENCH BLUEBERRY CREAM

Although a full-service restaurant, Betty's claim to fame will always be a wide variety of excellent pies.

Betty's Pies, a favorite stop for generations of North Shore travelers, began decades ago as a fish shack.

Split Rock Lighthouse: For Those in Peril on the Sea

It is beautiful, yes, but the reason it is there is tied to violent death and destruction. In the early twentieth century, weather forecasting was almost nonexistent. You could trust the aches in your knees to predict the weather as well as any current science. If you were a merchant seaman working the Great Lakes in those early days, it was never a question of avoiding a bad storm, only surviving it. Bad weather has existed since the dawn of time, but one particular weekend in 1905 was especially tragic for the sailors who plied the North Shore.

Today, they call it the Big Blow. On November 28, a fierce storm blew up on Lake Superior. Its winds reached over 80 miles per hour, hurling snow and ice into anything not sheltered. In one horrible, telling example, the steamer *John Stanton*, making for port, labored at full steam for 14 hours but made no forward progress. It was eventually blown into the rocks and lost.

In all, 29 ships were damaged or lost in less than 48 hours. A third of them were the property of U.S. Steel, and they were uninsured. At the time, U.S. Steel owned the largest fleet of freighters in the world, and moving iron ore from Lake Superior ore docks to steel mills in

A winding staircase leads to the top of the lighthouse.

These days, the foghorns at Split Rock operate at one-tenth of the volume they once used. Even so, it's enough to rattle your teeth.

The rocky shore of Lake Superior affords travelers a spectacular view of the Split Rock Lighthouse to the north.

Looking south from the top of Split Rock Lighthouse, the stunning shoreline of Lake Superior seems to go on forever.

As recently as the 1990s, Highway 61 used to cling to the cliffs overlooking Lake Superior. Eventually, engineers thought it would be safer to go through the mountain than over it. At 1,400 feet, the Silver Creek Cliff tunnel is one of the longest in the Midwest.

Tom's Logging Camp, a popular tourist attraction on the North Shore, re-creates the glory days of logging in the North Country.

Though much of the land in northern Minnesota is protected today, the logging industry is still vital and transports much of its product to market via the North Shore and Highway 61.

Father Frederick Baraga, the first bishop of Michigan's Upper Peninsula, was known as the "Snowshoe Priest" for his work with Native Americans around Lake Superior. This cross marks the spot where he landed after crossing Superior by canoe in 1846.

other Great Lakes ports was its greatest business. Soon after the Big Blow, company leaders arrived in Washington, D.C., with demands. In 1907, Congress approved a $75,000 allocation for a lighthouse and foghorn in the area.

It wasn't an enviable task, trying to build anything on the sheer 100-foot rock face, but in May 1909, they began. The first thing to go in was a huge derrick and hoisting engine; by the end of construction the following year, workers had hoisted more than 310 tons of materials atop the cliff.

The light itself was imported from France and assembled inside the tower. Gasoline-powered air compressors were built to run the foghorn. Houses and storage barns were built for the lighthouse keeper and his family.

On July 31, 1910, keeper Orren Young climbed the tower, 168 feet above the water of Lake Superior, and lit the oil vapor lamp at Split Rock for the first time. Every night, he and his successors did the same, beaming the light 20 miles out into the water. When visibility was limited by fog or snow, they started the foghorn, which was so deafening it frightened farm animals miles away.

In 1924, the North Shore Highway, aka Highway 61, was completed and tourists soon got a peek at the jewel of the lakeshore. The U.S. Coast Guard took over the operation of the lighthouse in 1939 and continued to tend it until it closed in 1969.

In 1971, the Minnesota Historical Society took possession of the site and has administered it ever since. Although the light hasn't been used since 1961, they employ a keeper in historical costume acting as a docent, and the foghorn is now run by an electric compressor and operates at one-tenth of its former volume. It is still enough to rattle your teeth.

In 1916, workers built a tramway down to the lake to haul supplies up the steep hillside. It was used until 1934, when supplies began arriving by truck. The tram is no longer there, but there is a wooden stairway that you can hike down to stroll the lakefront below. So I did.

There was a group of kids sitting on the lakeshore rocks and smoking a joint when I made it to the bottom.

A sign on the wall of a bait shop in Grand Marais, Minnesota, provides a not-so-subtle hint as to one of the region's most popular pastimes.

They quickly hopped to their feet and gave me the sort of stink-eye reserved for 40-something guys who happened to walk up and harsh their buzz. I gave them a wave and headed the other way down the shore. I sat back against a big rock and enjoyed the late-season sun before taking a few pictures and heading back.

Of course, what I failed to remember was what goes down must come up (with apologies to David Clayton Thomas). Even with the stairs, it was a long, slow, and steep climb back to the lighthouse, and about halfway up I recalled Cardiff Hill back in Hannibal, Missouri. There is a time in every man's life for climbing mountains because they are there. If my aching knees at the summit were any indication, that time in my life has passed.

I rolled out of the lighthouse parking lot and headed for Grand Marais, the last wide spot in the road before hitting the Grand Portage Indian Reservation, and soon thereafter, the Canadian border. Grand Marais' population is just over a thousand souls. It's a sleepy little burg, where the city hall doubles as the town liquor store and the mayor might well be the person behind the counter. There are plenty of things to do in the surrounding area, but aside from a few restaurants and shops, not much in the town itself. It seems a place people come to rest after a hard day of doing something somewhere else.

The Sea Wall Motel, like most other lodgings along Minnesota's North Shore, is a highly seasonal business.

The Minnesota Twins, in the process of winning a late-season game against the Chicago White Sox, get little attention inside a Grand Marais tavern.

Grand Portage: The Great Carrying Place

A bench in front of the storehouse at Grand Portage National Monument drinks in the October sun.

Along the lower Pigeon River, which separates Minnesota from Ontario, is a series of rapids and falls. Perhaps if you are headed downstream in a kayak with a belly full of Mountain Dew you might have a chance of making it through, but certainly not if you're going upstream in a birch-bark canoe with 20 men aboard.

Grand Portage, French for "great carrying place," is the name of a town, of a state park, and of the Indian reservation, but mostly it describes 9 miles of a ball-busting trail that bypassed the falls of the Pigeon River and dropped men at a fort upstream.

French-Canadian traders began arriving here in the middle of the seventeenth century and traded goods and lore with the Ojibwe and Cree tribes living in the area. These *voyageurs* (French for traveler) learned how to craft and repair their own canoes and how to survive the harsh North Country's brutal winters. They brought pieces of col-ored glass, iron tools, and wool blankets. In return they got furs by the ton.

Two distinct groups of voyageurs came to Grand Portage: the North Men and the Pork Eaters. The North Men would annually leave Grand Portage toward the end of July and paddle upstream, sometimes as far as the Great Slave Lake in what is now the Northwest Territories of Canada, before stopping to spend the winter trading with local tribes and amassing

The main room at Grand Portage was the site of formal functions hosted there by the North West Company. LIBRARY OF CONGRESS

Hundreds of years ago, this pier would have been lined with the huge birch canoes and stacked with pelts from the many VOYAGEURS *who passed through Grand Portage. Today, it seems the trappers have been replaced by visiting gulls. Signs at the head of the dock warn that Lake Superior's waters are icy, even during the summer, and that an accidental fall into the water could prove fatal.*

furs to take back the next spring. The Pork Eaters called Montreal home and, when the ice began to break in late May, would paddle west across the Great Lakes loaded with trade goods. The North Men would head back south as soon as the rivers were navigable and meet the Pork Eaters at the trading post in Grand Portage for an annual tradition—the *rendezvous*.

In its simplest sense, the rendezvous was about swapping fur for trinkets, with each group taking their spoils back home. The North Men kept the trinkets on hand to trade for furs the following winter; the Pork Eaters traded furs for cash back in Montreal. But the rendezvous was also a celebration of surviving another year in some of the most formidable terrain on earth. The North Men favored tents, the Pork Eaters slept under their canoes. There were many other differences between the two groups, and usually they came to a head at the rendezvous. There were fistfights and the liquor flowed until their money ran out. It was a party, but like any party, sooner or later it had to end. The two groups packed up and readied themselves for another cycle.

The fur trade at Grand Portage effectively ended 200 years ago, when the North West Company moved its headquarters to Fort William, outside the city limits of

what is today Thunder Bay, Ontario. But the old stockade is there, obviously rebuilt, but incredibly authentic all the same. The Great Hall, the dock, the warehouse, and the fur press are there, too, and like Old Fort Madison down in Iowa, there are re-enactors on hand to explain the lives and livelihoods of the voyageurs.

Each year, thousands of outdoorspeople access the Gunflint Trail and northeastern Minnesota's canoe country via downtown Grand Marais.

The reconstructed guardhouse at the Grand Portage National Monument.
LIBRARY OF CONGRESS

> *"With a load of iron ore twenty-six thousand tons more*
> *Than the Edmund Fitzgerald weighed empty,*
> *That good ship and true was a bone to be chewed*
> *When the gales of November came early."*
>
> —Gordon Lightfoot, "The Wreck of the Edmund Fitzgerald"

As I walked out of the stockade, there was a birch-bark canoe by the gate. At the dock, a sign warned me—in case I could have somehow forgotten—that this is Lake Superior and it is icy cold, even during the summer. If I was to fall in, it might well be fatal.

I walked to the end of the dock and sat down; my legs dangled a few inches above the icy water. I lit up a smoke and considered the lake before me.

This is a body of water that can rip an ore freighter in half, sending its cargo and crew to

On November 9, 1975, the ore freighter EDMUND FITZGERALD embarked from Superior Harbor near Duluth for Detroit with 26,116 tons of taconite pellets in its hold. The ship's captain, Ernest McSorley, was last heard from shortly after 7:00 the following evening. The FITZGERALD sunk after failing to make safe harbor in the midst of a ferocious storm—all 29 men on board perished. Immortalized in song by Gordon Lightfoot, the freighter is shown here less than six months before it sank. UNIVERSITY OF WISCONSIN-SUPERIOR. JIM DAN HILL LIBRARY. PHOTO BY BOB CAMPBELL

Gordon Lightfoot had a long history as a respected Canadian folksinger before he struck both the American psyche and solid gold with "The Wreck of the Edmund Fitzgerald." While the song has fallen into the oldies canon, to stand on the shore of GITCHIGUMEE, *as the Ojibwe refer to Lake Superior, and hear the words "Superior, it's said, never gives up her dead" echo in your mind, is like having ice water poured down your back. However maudlin the song has become, it is one of the best and last examples of a folk song—a true relation of a factual incident—making it onto the Top 40 charts.* COURTESY REPRISE RECORDS

The Beaver House, located across the street from Grand Marais City Hall, offers maps, movie rentals, and live bait.

The main drag in Grand Marais on a sunny autumn afternoon.

a silent death. I thought of the line from Gordon Lightfoot, "Superior, it's said, never gives up her dead" . . . apparently true. Since the water is so cold, a body does not decay and produce the gases that bloat it and raise it to the surface.

"How many?" I thought. We know that all 29 men aboard the *Edmund Fitzgerald* died, but how many times has that happened on this lake—100, 200 times? What kind of man did it take to get in a canoe made out of glorified papier-mâché and paddle off into what he knew would be either certain death or bone-crushing hardship?

An odd thought came back to me as I sat on the dock. I am half Canadian, and I remember when I was a child my mother told me about an uncle, or cousin, or third cousin once removed, or whatever the hell it was, who lived in Yellowknife on the Great Slave Lake. I couldn't remember his name for the life of me. He was a North Man by god, not descended from the originals— my people didn't show up in this hemisphere until the late nineteenth century—but a North Man all the same. Whatever his name was, I thought of him as I got back in the van and turned north, heading for Canada.

Bill Bally's old blacksmith shop in Grand Marais is on the National Register of Historic Places.

A pair of sailboats waits out the end of the season in the protected harbor at Grand Marais.

The sunset paints vivid colors in the sky over Grand Marais as the tourist season draws to a close.

The falls at Pigeon River, which separates Minnesota from Ontario and flows under Highway 61 on its way to Lake Superior, plummet 120 feet and prompted the native Ojibwe to forge a 9-mile bypass. French-Canadian fur traders later dubbed the trail "Grand Portage." Today the falls lie within Grand Portage State Park, the only such state facility that comprises land leased from the Bureau of Indian Affairs. MINNESOTA OFFICE OF TOURISM

Behind our house there is a pond,
Fal la de ra.
There came three beautiful ducks to swim thereon . . .
The prince to chase them he did run,
Fal la de ra.
And he had his great silver gun . . .

—*"En roulant ma boule" ("A-Rolling My Ball"), traditional voyageur folk song*

This bird has flown . . . perhaps to elude the prince
with his great silver gun. As the season winds down
on the North Shore, a mallard departs the harbor
at Grand Marais for warmer climes.

Epilogue

I pulled up to the Canadian Port of Entry and rolled down my window. At the gate, a pleasant-looking chap of maybe 30 shoved back his window and grinned.

"How long ya gonna be in Canada then, eh?" he asked.

"'Bout 10 minutes, I guess. I'm shooting pictures for this kind of book," I answered. "I just need to find a sign that says, 'Welcome to Canada' or 'Highway 61 Ontario' or something, and take a picture of it. Is there something like that up ahead?"

"Hell, I dunno," he laughed. "There's some kind of tourism stand up the way, huh? You can check with them."

"OK, will do," I called, driving off with a wave. And that was it.

About a half-mile up the road was a blue-and-white sign that read, "Welcome to Ontario." I got out and snapped a shot of it. I turned the camera around to take the shot at a different angle and exposure but got nothing. I looked down at the camera and realized my battery was dead. I pulled a U-turn in the grassy median and headed back for the United States.

I slowed to a stop as I got to the U.S. Port of Entry.

"How long have you been in Canada, sir?" asked a female customs agent.

"About five minutes" I answered. By this time, another customs agent was at my passenger window, craning his head inside, looking around the van's interior.

"Yeah?" she said. "So what did you do there?"

"Took a picture," I said, feeling that the truth would only baffle these folks.

"So what do you do for a living, sir?" she asked, gesturing to the other agent.

"Right now, I take pictures," I answered, with a dreadful feeling that the truth was not going to set me free when dealing with a couple of piss-ant federal employees.

"Do me a favor," the first agent said with a grin. "Give me your driver's license and pull in right over here."

Wonderful. After searching the van, finding absolutely nothing but maps, camera equipment, and empty film cans, and running my data through every criminal database known to the Western World, they let me go.

I stopped in Grand Marais long enough to get a new camera battery and headed back south. I don't know how many hours later it was, but I pulled into my friends' place in La Crosse, Wisconsin, and switched off the motor. It was dark out.

The next morning, as I warmed up the van on my way back to Chicago, I flipped on the AM radio news station I had found on the way up. Everything north of Duluth was experiencing a sudden and violent winter storm, the first of the season.

I came home.

The fat lady has sung. Just north of the Ojibwe tribal lands, the Canadian border welcomes.

Resources and Bibliography

Useful Address and Internet Links

Sam's Place
1120 Tulane Avenue
New Orleans, LA 70125

Hot Biscuits Recording Company
221 Metairie Court
Metairie, LA 70001
www.hackberryramblers.com

The Myrtles Plantation
7747 Highway 61
St. Francisville, LA 70775
www.myrtlesplantation.com

Butler Greenwood Plantation
8345 Highway 61
St. Francisville, LA 70775
www.butlergreenwood.com

Vicksburg National Battlefield
3201 Clay Street
Vickburg, MS 39183
www.nps.gov.vick

Shack Up Inn
Hopson Plantation
001 Commisary Circle
Clarksdale, MS 38614
www.shackupinn.com

Riverside Hotel
615 Sunflower Avenue
Clarksdale, MS 38614

Graceland
3734 Elvis Presley Blvd.
Memphis, TN 38186
www.elvis.com

National Civil Rights Museum (Lorraine Motel)
450 Mulberry St.
Memphis, TN 38103
www.civilrightsmuseum.org

Lansky Brothers
Peabody Hotel
149 Union Street
Memphis, TN 38103
www.lanskybros.com

The Gideons International
2900 Lebanon Road
Nashville, TN 37214
www.gideons.org

Lambert's Café
2515 East Malone
Sikeston, MO 63801
www.throwedrolls.com

Mark Twain Boyhood Home and Museum
208 Hill Street
Hannibal, MO 63401
www.marktwainmuseum.org

Old Fort Madison
Highway 61 and Riverview Park
Fort Madison, IA 52627
www.oldfortmadison.com

The Dickeyville Grotto
Highway 151 and West Main.
Dickeyville, WI 53808

The *Julia Belle Swain*
227 Main Street
La Crosse, WI 54601
www.juliabelle.com

A Prairie Home Companion
611 Frontenac Place
St. Paul, MN 55104
www.prairiehome.org

X-Communication Publishing
1002 North Thirteenth Avenue East
Duluth, MN 55805
www.x-communication.org

Grand Portage National Monument
211 Mile Creek Road
Grand Portage, MN 5566
www.nps.gov/grpo

Recommended Reading

Butler, Anne. *Weep for the Living* (Xlibris Corporation, 2000)

Dierckins, Tony and Kerry Elliott. *True North: Alternate and Off-Beat Destinations in and Around*

Duluth, Superior, and the Shores of Lake Superior (Bad Dog Press, 2003)

Dylan, Bob. *Lyrics, 1962–2002* (Simon & Schuster, 2004)

Engel, Dave. *Just Like Bob Zimmerman's Blues: Dylan in Minnesota* (Amherst Press, 1999)

Feichtinger, Gail. *Will to Murder: The True Story behind the Crimes & Trials Surrounding the Glensheen Killings* (X-Communication, 2003)

Fitzgerald, F. Scott. *Novels and Stories, 1920–1922* (Library of America, 2000)

Florence, Robert and Mason Florence. *New Orleans Cemeteries* (Batture Press, 1997)

Grant, Ulysses S. and Mary Drake and William S. McFeely, eds. *Memoirs and Selected Letters, 1839–1865* (Library of America, 1990)

Guralnick, Peter. *Careless Love: The Umaking of Elvis Presley* (Little, Brown & Company, 1999)

———. *Last Train to Memphis: The Rise of Elvis Presley* (Little Brown & Company, 1994)

———. *Lost Highway: Journeys and Arrivals of American Musicians* (Back Bay Books reprint, 1999)

———. *Searching for Robert Johnson* (Obelisk, 1989)

Guralnick, Peter and Robert Santelli. *Martin Scorsese Presents the Blues: A Musical Journey* (Amistad Press, 2003)

Hankinson, Alan and David G. Chandler, ed. *Vicksburg 1863: Grant Clears the Mississippi (Campaign No. 26)* (Osprey Publishing Company, 1993)

Keillor, Garrison. *Lake Wobegon Days* (Viking Press, 1999)

Lomax, Alan. *The Land Where the Blues Began* (Pantheon Books, 1993)

McKeen, William and Graham McKeen. *Highway 61: A Father-and-Son Journey through the Middle of America* (W. W. Norton & Company, 2003)

Niles, Susan A. *The Dickeyville Grotto: The Vision of Father Mathias Wernerus* (University Press of Mississippi, 1997)

Olivier, Rick and Ben Sandmel. *Zydeco!* (University Press of Mississippi, 1999)

Palmer, Robert. *Deep Blues* (Viking Press, 1995)

Ripsaw News (www.ripsawnews.com)

Smith, Michael Peter and Ben Sandmel. *New Orleans Jazz Fest: A Pictorial History* (Pelican Publishing Company, 1991)

Twain, Mark and Louis J. Budd, ed. *Collected Tales, Sketches, Speeches & Essays, 1852–1890* (Library of America, 1992)

Twain, Mark and Guy Cardwell, ed. *Mississippi Writings* (Library of America, 1982)

Welty, Eudora. *Complete Novels* (Library of America, 1998)

———. *Photographs* (University Press of Mississippi, 1989)

———. *Stories, Essays & Memoir* (Library of America, 1998)

Essential Listening

Berry, Chuck. *The Great Twenty-Eight* (MCA, 1982)

Biederbecke, Bix. *Bix* (Tristar, 1994)

Bottle Rockets. *Bottle Rockets* (East Side Digital, 1993)

———. *The Brooklyn Side* (East Side Digital, 1994)

———. *24 Hours a Day* (Atlantic, 1997)

———. *Blue Sky* (Sanctuary, 2003)

Chikan, Super. *Shoot That Thang* (Rooster Blues, 2000)

———. *What You See* (Fat Possum, 2001)

Dr. John. *The Very Best of Dr. John* (Rhino, 1995)

Dylan, Bob. *Bob Dylan* (Columbia, 1962)

———. *The Freewheelin' Bob Dylan* (Columbia, 1963)

———. *Bringing It All Back Home* (Columbia, 1965)

———. *Highway 61 Revisited* (Columbia, 1965)

———. *John Wesley Harding* (Columbia, 1968)

———. *Nashville Skyline* (Columbia, 1969)

———. *Self Portrait* (Columbia, 1970)

Edwards, David "Honeyboy". *Mississippi Delta Bluesman* (Smithsonian Folkways, 2001)

Farrar, Jay. *Sebastopol* (Fellow Guard/Artemis, 2001)

———. *Terroir Blues* (Act/Resist, 2003)

Gaillard, Slim. *1938–1946* (Best of Jazz, 1999)

Green, Al. *Greatest Hits* (Capitol, 1975)

Hackberry Ramblers, The. *Deep Water* (Hot Biscuits, 1997)

———. *Early Recordings 1935–1950* (Arhoolie, 2003)

House, Son. *Complete Library of Congress Sessions* (Travelin' Man, 1996)

———. *1928–1930* (Document, 1994)

Hurt, Mississippi John. *Avalon Blues: The Complete 1928 Okeh Recordings* (Sony, 1996)

Johnson, Johnnie. *Johnnie B. Bad* (Nonesuch, 1991)

Johnson, Robert. *The Complete Recordings* (Columbia Records, 1990)

Keillor, Garrison. *A Prairie Home Companion: 25th Anniversary Collection* (Highbridge Company, 1999)

King, B. B. *Do The Boogie! B. B. King's Early '50s Classics* (Virgin, 1988)

———. *Greatest Hits* (MCA, 1998)

Lightfoot, Gordon. *Complete Greatest Hits* (Rhino, 2002)

McDowell, Mississippi Fred. *Mississippi Fred McDowell* (Rounder 1971)
———. *I Do Not Play No Rock 'n' Roll* (Varese, 2001)

Meters, The. *The Very Best of the Meters* (Rhino, 1997)

Nighthawk, Robert. *Bricks in My Pillow* (Pearl Flapper, 1977)

Patton, Charlie. *Founder of the Delta Blues* (Yazoo, 1995)

Perkins, Pinetop. *The Complete High Tone Sessions* (High Tone, 2003)

Presley, Elvis. *The Sun Sessions* (RCA, 1976)

Smith, Bessie. *Empty Bed Blues* (ASV/Living Era, 1996)

Son Volt. *Trace* (Warner Brothers, 1995)

Uncle Tupelo. *No Depression* (Rockville, 1990)

———. *Still Feel Gone* (Rockville, 1991)

———. *March 16–20, 1992* (Rockville, 1992)

———. *Anodyne* (Sire/Reprise, 1993)

Various. *The Mississippi: River of Song* (Smithsonian Folkways, 1998)

———. *Duluth Does Dylan* (Spinout, 2000)

———. *Martin Scorsese Presents the Best of the Blues* (UTV Records, 2003)

Williamson, Sonny Boy. *Bring Another Half Pint* (Recall Records, 2000)

Wolf, Howlin'. *His Best: Chess 50th Anniversary Collection* (MCA, 1997)

———. *The London Howlin' Wolf Sessions* (Chess, 1971)

Index

Index

Index

Acknowledgments

No matter what it says on the cover, a project like this does not come together without some help along the way. A lot of folks went above and beyond the call of duty while helping me track down photographs, phone numbers, stories, people, and the nearest cold beer. Although I am loathe to make these sorts of lists for fear of forgetting someone, here, in no particular order, are just a few of the people who helped me get this piece of cheese done:

Howard Stovall, Anne Butler, Rat and Nate at the Riverside Hotel, Super Chikan, BJ Johnson at Lambert's Café, Mr. Bernard J. Lansky, Hal Lansky, Joan Collins (not the skanky English one), Captain Carl Henry, Laura Jolley, Dr. Dennis Ciesielski, Dr. Virginia Crank, Kip Welborn, the Memphis Police Department, Tina Keenan, Ben Sandmel, Julia and Peter at Mondovox Design, Shellee Graham (el photobabe numero uno), Jim Ross at *American Road* magazine, Cadillac Dave for being "the man" in the truest Velvet Underground sense of the word, my agent Sterling Lord, Steve LaVere, Tony Dierckins, Tim Nelson at Spinout Records, Chris Monroe, Eric Dregni and Mark Vesley, Sharon Marsh at Act/Resist, Scott Coopwood at the *Delta Business Journal,* Henry Sweet, Jon Robinson, John Koharski, Cathy Morrison and Gary Reinhart at MoDOT, webguy extraordinaire Jeff Behnke, Jodie Thomas at Artemis Records, Jay Farrar (wherever he is), Brian Henneman and Diesel Island, Fred Friction and the staff of Fredrick's Musical Lounge, the staff of the Front Street Brewery, Ron Warnick and Emily Priddy, Eric and PK, and Kenny J.

Special thanks to Dennis Pernu, a keen editor who has fostered this project from the beginning with insight, understanding, and great restraint in not actually cutting the definition of the word "deadline" out of the dictionary, enlarging it a thousandfold, and pasting it to a billboard outside my office window.

And most importantly, a large wet sloppy Jim Beam–breathed kiss to Jim Luning for driving the van, shooting photos, and going my bail. Repeatedly.

Author Tim Steil (left) and photographer Jim Luning (below) photographed in Memphis, Tennessee, 2002. JIM LUNING